Life of Christ

daily bread
:een bible studies

LIFE OF CHRIST

The Synoptic Gospels

FLORIDA COLLEGE
PRESS

Life of Christ: The Synoptic Gospels
Daily Bread Teen Bible Studies
Copyright © 2025

Florida College Press
119 N. Glen Arven Ave.
Temple Terrace, Florida 33617

ISBN: 978-1-965356-06-7

Printed in the United States of America.

Images for the cover and the lessons from various artists at pexels.com

CONTENTS

HOW TO USE THIS STUDY

As physical creatures, we regularly find food in the pantry for snacks. We tend to eat several meals a day of various sizes. Most of us have foods we love, foods we abhor, and foods we tolerate because we know they are good for us. Personally, I'm happy to grab a bowl full of Doritos and a big glass of sweet tea. I know these are bad for me and will lead me further down the road towards an expanded waistline, but they taste good. I also despise celery sticks.

In these daily bread studies, we seek to feast on God's Word as if it is the food that sustains our lives. Spiritually speaking, it is. Like lunch is for the body, scripture is for the soul. Statistically, about 90% of Americans own a Bible. Most of those homes own multiple copies of the Bible. Yet, only around 20% of those Bible owners have actually read the entire Bible. They own it, but they treat it like celery sticks.

Quoting that same source, it says:

> Americans also differ in how they approach reading the Bible. Twenty-two percent read a little bit each day, in a systematic approach. A third (35 percent) never pick it up at all, while 30 percent look up things in the Bible when they need to. Nineteen percent re-read their favorite parts, while 17 percent flip open the Bible and read a randomly chosen passage. A quarter (27 percent) read sections suggested by others, while 16 percent say they look things up to help others.

This is a problem. God's people should read God's Word. God's people should consume the Bible more sustainably than Doritos but more enjoyably than a dreaded vegetable. It should be a meal with enjoyable and healthy options—enough with the food analogy.

This series of studies aims to help young people develop an appetite for God's Word (there I go again with food). We want to create habits that will stay with them for the rest of their lives. We want them to learn to not only read through texts and ask good questions but also find things in the text when they need them.

We designed these books so people could take them home and study seven days a week. Sunday allows the student to read a quick overview of the lesson, followed by a short Bible reading Monday through Saturday. Each day, there are a few questions about the text to help the student think deeper. At the end of each lesson is a series of questions that can help you think through more complicated questions. At the end of the book, there is a short explanation for each of those questions to point the student in the right direction in case they get stuck.

Our goal is to help the student study the entire New Testament in textual and topical studies. If students do this, they will develop great habits and learn much about what the New Testament teaches about the Kingdom of God and our place in it.

It is our prayer that each of us, adult and teen, better learn to feast on God's Word. No matter how often you go through it, you will find new details that fascinate you all over again. Like any good meal, there is much to enjoy, even if you've had it before. No one turns up their nose at ribeye steak just because they've had it before. They go and enjoy a feast again. We hope you will use the Daily Bible study series to feast on repeat. We pray it will bless you with incredible spiritual health and enjoyment.

It might be too much to say, as John said, "Beloved, I pray that in all respects you may prosper and be in good health, just as your soul prospers." What would we look like if our physical bodies only prospered as our spiritual bodies did? If we placed physical prosperity on the same level as spiritual prosperity, would we feel and look healthy? We pray that this study will make that possible for you, even if you are one who struggles as a Bible student. God has given us what we need in His word, and our prayer for you in this study is that you take advantage of this and your soul prospers greatly.

COMPLETE (ADDITIONAL) READING SCHEDULE

The most important part of this study is developing a habit of reading the Bible every day. This reading schedule is designed to help you not only open your Bible every day but also read a portion. The daily lessons will include short readings specific to the questions being asked.

This reading schedule is provided as an additional reading and will help you read all of Matthew, Mark, and Luke through the twelve weeks of this study. Because this reading schedule spreads the reading over the entire twelve weeks, these readings do not match up with your daily lessons, yet one chapter a day gets it done. We recommend that you read in the morning and do your lesson in the evening, or vice versa. The important goal is to get into the Word of God more regularly. We hope you will diligently develop good habits. Through these twelve weeks, you'll learn a lot about your diligence and what works best for you as you continue forward as a student.

Week 1

o	Day 1	Matthew 1	o	Day 4	Luke 2
o	Day 2	Luke 1	o	Day 5	Matthew 3
o	Day 3	Matthew 2	o	Day 6	Luke 3

Week 2

o	Day 1	Matthew 4	o	Day 4	Matthew 5
o	Day 2	Luke 4	o	Day 5	Matthew 6
o	Day 3	Mark 1	o	Day 6	Matthew 7

Week 3

- o Day 1 Luke 5
- o Day 2 Luke 6
- o Day 3 Mark 2
- o Day 4 Matthew 8
- o Day 5 Mark 3
- o Day 6 Luke 7

Week 4

- o Day 1 Matthew 9
- o Day 2 Mark 4
- o Day 3 Luke 8
- o Day 4 Matthew 10
- o Day 5 Mark 5
- o Day 6 Luke 9

Week 5

- o Day 1 Matthew 11
- o Day 2 Luke 10
- o Day 3 Mark 6
- o Day 4 Matthew 12
- o Day 5 Luke 11
- o Day 6 Mark 7

Week 6

- o Day 1 Matthew 13
- o Day 2 Mark 8
- o Day 3 Luke 12
- o Day 4 Matthew 14
- o Day 5 Mark 9
- o Day 6 Luke 13

Week 7

- o Day 1 Matthew 15
- o Day 2 Mark 10
- o Day 3 Luke 14
- o Day 4 Matthew 16
- o Day 5 Matthew 17
- o Day 6 Luke 15

Week 8

- o Day 1 Matthew 18
- o Day 2 Luke 16
- o Day 3 Matthew 19
- o Day 4 Luke 17
- o Day 5 Matthew 20
- o Day 6 Luke 18

Week 9

- o Day 1 Mark 11
- o Day 2 Matthew 21
- o Day 3 Luke 19
- o Day 4 Matthew 22
- o Day 5 Mark 12
- o Day 6 Luke 20

Week 10

- o Day 1   Matthew 23   o Day 4   Matthew 24
- o Day 2   Mark 13   o Day 5   Matthew 25
- o Day 3   Luke 21   o Day 6   Matthew 26

Week 11

- o Day 1   Mark 14   o Day 4   John 14
- o Day 2   Luke 22   o Day 5   John 15
- o Day 3   John 13   o Day 6   John 16

Week 12

- o Day 1   Matthew 27   o Day 4   Matthew 28
- o Day 2   Mark 15   o Day 5   Mark 16
- o Day 3   Luke 23   o Day 6   Luke 24

PRESTUDY THOUGHT QUESTIONS

1 Does Jesus matter? Why?

2 Who is Jesus in your own words?

3 What story about Jesus most stands out in your memory?

4 What does Jesus mean for us today?

5 Is Jesus the Messiah? Explain.

6 Is Jesus the Son of God? Explain.

7 What does it mean for Jesus to be both God and man?

8 Are the Gospels (Matthew, Mark, Luke, and John) reliable historical accounts?

9 Why do the Gospels share so many similarities and stories?

10 Why do the Gospels have so many differences?

11 If you wanted to convince a friend that Jesus was worth their time, how would you do it? What would you say?

12 If Jesus is King and Lord, what does that require of us? Do you act as if Jesus is King and Lord?

13 Jesus was amazing, but He was also very real. When you think of Jesus, do you think of Him in real terms, or as a character in a book?

14 God can do anything anyway He wants to. Why send Jesus, knowing Jesus would suffer and die?

Therefore, the Lord himself will give you a sign: See, the virgin will conceive, have a son, and name him Immanuel.
Isaiah 7.1

WEEK 1

BIRTH

THE BIRTH OF A SAVIOR

> *Complete Reading:*
> *Matthew 1-3, Luke 1-3*

The world was a mess. Wars had raged for centuries between nations. The Israelites were often in the middle of these wars, not by choice but because of geography. The Romans hated the Jews, and the feeling was mutual.

God had promised a savior would come since man was in the Garden of Eden, and the Jewish people expected it to happen any day. The prophets promised a king, a priest, a ruler, and ultimately peace, but the Jewish people wanted a king to defeat their enemies and rule over them. Yet, God had a different plan.

This plan began with the "forerunner" of the Savior who would come in the likeness of Elijah.[1] Zechariah, a priest, was promised he would have a son, but he struggled to believe because he and his wife Elizabeth were old. The angel Gabriel struck him mute until he believed.

God sent another message supernaturally to Mary through the voice of an angel who calls her "Blessed among women." "You will conceive and give birth to a son, and you will name him Jesus. He will be great and will be called the Son of the Most High, and the Lord God will give him the throne of his father David. He will reign over the house of Jacob forever, and his kingdom will have no end."[2] This is the message the Jews wanted, but it was not happening the way they wanted. They wanted a warrior, but God sent a baby.

An angel also appeared to Joseph, who was engaged to marry Mary. He was unsure what to think, but knowing that she was pregnant

---

1   Malachi 4.5-6
2   Luke 1.28, 31-33

and that the baby was not his, he seems to have assumed the worst. He did not wish to harm her, so he planned to put her away quietly, but the angel assured him that Mary was still innocent even though she was pregnant.

Joseph and Mary seemed to think it would be best if Mary went to stay with Elizabeth, her cousin, while Elizabeth was in the final stages of her pregnancy. She was older and could certainly use the help. When Mary arrived, the baby John leapt in Elizabeth's womb, and Elizabeth declared Mary blessed among women. In a moment of clarity, Elizabeth proclaims that Mary's baby is her Lord. Mary responds with a prayer that has come to be called the Magnificat. She proclaims praise to God, who is the help of Israel and the despised. Mary stays with Elizabeth for three months, and eventually, John is born and named by his father, who is then able to speak again. He gives his prophecy once he can talk again and declares that God is finally rescuing His people.

"The birth of Jesus made possible not just a new way of understanding life but a new way of living it."
- F. Buchner

The time came for Mary to have her baby, and she and her betrothed Joseph were forced to travel from their home in Nazareth to Bethlehem for a Roman census. When they arrived, so did the baby. They could find no place to stay in a town that was not their home, and they ended up being pointed to a stable or a common place where animals could come and where there was no privacy. In the squalor of animal messes and feeding troughs, Jesus was born into the world. This mixed animal sounds with the sounds of a baby's cry and mixed the smells of a baby with a barn.

Consider how humiliating this entire nine months would be for Mary and Joseph. They were unmarried but pregnant. She was innocent and a virgin, but the world would assume otherwise. Joseph would have lost all respect by those who assumed wrong-doing. They would be considered liars when they told the truth that their baby was from God. They would have been considered shameful, ostracized by their family and friends, and despised by their community. It was probably an easy choice for them not to return to Nazareth after the census. Instead, they made their home in Bethlehem.

When they were to have the baby finally, there was no place in the town for their family. They laid the Savior of the nation in the hay. The newborn king had no throne nor even a bed. Only a few dirty shepherds came to worship when the baby was born after hearing from a chorus of angels singing of his birth. No kings arrive. No dignitaries acknowledge the newborn King of kings. The Bread of Life is wrapped in cloth and lying where cows and goats have eaten. The Creator is now one of the creations. The One on whom all mankind depends entirely depends on the mothering skills of one who has never been a mother, never known a man, never been responsible for her own life, much less a baby.

The whole event is humiliating on a human level, and even more so when we consider the true identity of this baby. Yet, it demonstrates the character of a God who likes to thwart the expectations of His creation. He has a history of doing the unexpected, making heroes out of the unlikely, and saving the helpless through unlikely means. God can do the impossible by bringing "peace on earth" and showing "goodwill towards men."

MESSIANIC PROPHECIES
THE BIRTH OF JESUS

Therefore, the Lord himself will give you a sign: See, the virgin will conceive, have a son, and name him Immanuel (Isa 7.14).	**BORN OF A VIRGIN**	The angel replied to her, "... Therefore, the holy one to be born will be called the Son of God (Luke 1.35).
Therefore, the Lord himself will give you a sign: See, the virgin will conceive, have a son, and name him Immanuel (Isa 7.14).	**CALLED IMMANUEL**	Now all this took place to fulfill what was spoken... **they will name him Immanuel,** which is translated "God is with us" (Matthew 1.22-23).
I will bless those who bless you, I will curse anyone who treats you with contempt, and all the peoples on earth will be blessed through you (Gen 12.3).	**LINEAGE OF ABRAHAM**	God raised up his servantand sent him first to you to bless you by turning each of you from your evil ways (Acts 3.25-26).
Your offspring will be like the dust of the earth, and you will spread out toward the west, the east, the north, and the south. All the peoples on earth will be blessed through you and your offspring (Gen 28.14).	**LINEAGE OF JUDAH**	An account of the genealogy of Jesus Christ..., Isaac fathered Jacob (Matthew 1.1-2).
The scepter will not depart from Judah or the staff from between his feet until he whose right it is comes and the obedience of the peoples belongs to him (Gen 49.10).	**A PROMISED KING**	son of Judah, son of Jacob, son of Isaac, son of Abraham, (Luk 3.33-34).
When your time comes and you rest with your ancestors, I will raise up after you your descendant, who will come from your body, and I will establish his kingdom. He is the one who will build a house for my name, and I will establish the throne of his kingdom forever (2 Sam 7.12-13).	**LINEAGE OF DAVID**	An account of the genealogy of Jesus Christ, the Son of David, the Son of Abraham: (Matthew 1.1).
Bethlehem Ephrathah, you are small among the clans of Judah; one will come from you to be ruler over Israel for me. His origin is from antiquity, from ancient times (Micah 5.2).	**BORN IN BETHLEHEM**	So he... asked them where the Messiah would be born. "In Bethlehem of Judea," they told him... (Matthew 2.4-6).

THE ANNOUNCEMENTS OF GABRIEL

SCRIPTURES: LUKE 1.1-20, 21-38; MATTHEW 1.18-25

Zechariah received a message from Gabriel. What was it?

Mary received a message from Gabriel. What was it?

What compliments did the angel say about Mary?

Joseph received a message in a dream. What was it?

THE BIRTH OF JOHN

SCRIPTURES: LUKE 1.21-25, 57-80

What were John's father's and mother's names?

What did the angel say was significant about John?

On what day was John named? What else happened that day?

What significant role did Zechariah's prophesy that John would do in his life?

GENEALOGY OF JESUS

SCRIPTURES: MATTHEW 1.1-17

Why do you think Matthew begins his genealogy with Abraham?

The first section is from Abraham to David. Name your favorite story from this part of the Bible.

The second section is from David to the exile to Babylon. Name your favorite story from this section of Bible history.

The third section begins after the exile to the time of Jesus. Have you heard of any of the people from this section?

THE BIRTH OF JESUS

SCRIPTURES: LUKE 2.1-20

Joseph took Mary from Nazareth to Bethlehem. Why?

Where was there no room for Joseph and Mary?

The angels appeared to the shepherds. What were they told?

Write out verse 19 below.

PROPHECIES ABOUT JESUS

SCRIPTURES: LISTED BELOW

Below are several prophecies concerning Jesus. Read these scriptures and identify how this is fulfilled in Jesus. If possible, give a New Testament passage that identifies this being fulfilled:

I will bless those who bless you,

I will curse anyone who treats you with contempt,

and all the peoples on earth

will be blessed through you (Genesis 12.3).

The scepter will not depart from Judah

or the staff from between his feet

until he whose right it is comes

and the obedience of the peoples

belongs to him (Genesis 49.10).

PROPHECIES ABOUT JESUS

SCRIPTURES: LISTED BELOW

Below are several prophecies concerning Jesus. Read these scriptures and identify how this is fulfilled in Jesus. If possible, give a New Testament passage that identifies this being fulfilled:

Therefore, the Lord himself will give you a sign:

See, the virgin will conceive, have a son,

and name him Immanuel (Isaiah 7.14).

Bethlehem Ephrathah,

you are small among the clans of Judah;

one will come from you

to be ruler over Israel for me.

His origin is from antiquity,

from ancient times (Micah 5.2).

DEEPER THINKING QUESTIONS

1 Why was Zechariah chosen to be the father of John? What does this mean for us today?

2 Why did Zechariah struggle to believe the message of the angel? How would you have responded in his situation?

3 The angel's message to Zechariah was full of positive ideas. List some below.

4 Name other stories in the Bible that are similar to the story of Zechariah and Elizabeth.

5 What does the angel call Mary? What does this mean?

6 Why did Mary struggle to believe the message of the angel?

7 Compare Mary's song to the song of Hannah in 1 Samuel 2.1-10.

8 The angel's message to Mary was full of positive and negative ideas. List some of the negative.

9 What would you have done in Joseph's shoes considering the difficulty of the situation? Explain your answer.

10 What would have been the hardest part of the nativity story?

11 When the angels appeared to the shepherds, what did they proclaim?

12 How did the shepherds feel when the angels appeared? Name other stories in the Bible where people had this same reaction to angels.

13 When we see the many prophecies fulfilled by Jesus's birth, how should we respond to Jesus's birth?

14 Name the women mentioned in Jesus's genealogy in Matthew 1. Why is this significant?

NOTES

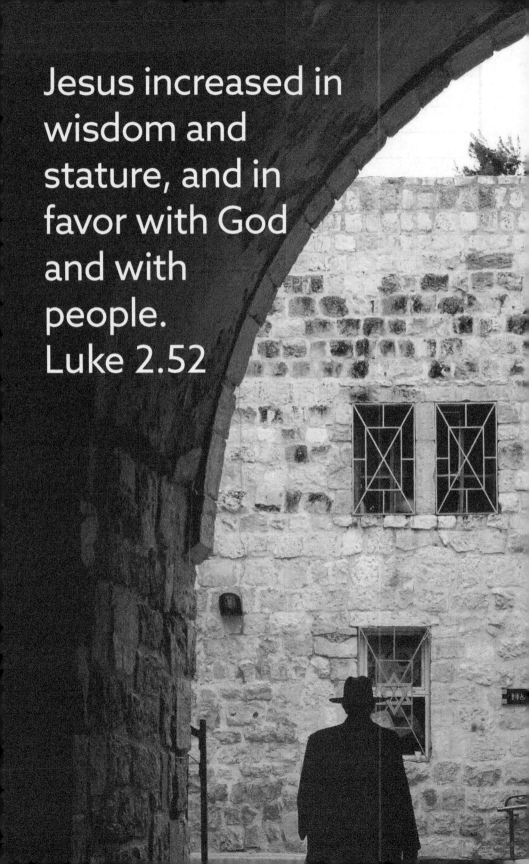

Jesus increased in wisdom and stature, and in favor with God and with people.
Luke 2.52

YOUTH

THE YOUNG MAN JESUS

Complete Reading:
Matthew 4-7; Mark 1; Luke 4

Mary was favored by God. Joseph was her betrothed. These two were inarguably the most important set of parents that ever lived, chosen by God Himself to raise God's Son. Immediately following Jesus's birth, we see evidence of why. Jesus is named on the eighth day at the time of his circumcision.[1] At the time of their purification, they went to Jerusalem as the Law directed.[2] They brought him because they were dedicating him to the Lord.[3] We read later that they went to Jerusalem for the feasts. These two parents were dedicated to God and were going to raise Jesus similarly.

The baby Jesus, at a little over a month old, was carried to the temple for dedication. Joseph and Mary offer a pair of birds, the only sacrifice they can afford. While in Jerusalem, they meet a man named Simeon, who the Holy Spirit has told that he would not die until he saw the Messiah. When he sees Jesus, the Spirit reveals to him that Jesus is the one. He praised God while holding Jesus with words of praise, calling Jesus God's salvation. He tells Mary, "Indeed, this child is destined to cause the fall and rise of many in Israel and to be a sign that will be opposed – and a sword will pierce your own soul–that the thoughts of many hearts may be revealed."[4] They also meet Anna, an aged woman who has been praying for the Savior, and she thanks God for bringing the redemption of Jerusalem.

Sometime later, after Joseph and Mary found a home in Bethlehem,

---

1   The law concerning circumcision is given to Abraham in Genesis 17.
2   This law is found in the Mosaic Law in Leviticus 12.
3   This command is found in Exodus 13.2, 13-15; 22.28-29.
4   Luke 2.34-35

some men from the East showed up. Some versions call them wise men; others call them magi, and others call them kings. We know they were men of prominence. They noticed a star in the sky that revealed to them that a king had been born in the west. They decided to follow that star and find the king.[5] They followed it to Judea and asked the sitting king, Herod the Great, where they could find the new king. He asked his wise men who knew the Law, and they revealed that the king would come from Bethlehem.[6] He asked the wise men to come back and tell him once they found the king so he could also go and pay homage. They continued their search and came to Jesus carrying gifts of gold, frankincense, and myrrh and offered worship to this new king proclaimed by the stars. God warned them in a dream not to reveal the location to Herod, so they went home instead.

"Jesus Christ: The meeting place of eternity and time, the blending of deity and humanity, the junction of heaven and earth."
- Anonymous

This made Herod angry, jealous, and scared, so he decided to eliminate the boy king. He only knew that this child would be in Bethlehem, so he decreed that all boys, two years old and younger, be slaughtered. Herod's insecurity caused mass murder. God sends an angel to tell Joseph to take Mary and Jesus to Egypt to escape the massacre and to stay there until he is told to bring them back. They immediately get up and flee Israel. They remained in this foreign land until Herod died.

When Herod's son, Archelaus, became the new king, Joseph brought Mary and Jesus back to Israel. Instead of returning to Bethlehem, they went to Nazareth, a city in Galilee, outside of Archelaus's territory.

Years pass, and when Jesus is twelve, his family takes a trip to

---

5   Whether following a star was a physical following of the star's movement or following the message of the star when combined with other information is unclear in the text.

6   Revealed in Micah 5.2

Jerusalem to celebrate the Passover feast, their annual custom. When they start home, at the end of the first day, they find Jesus is missing. Not finding him in their caravan, they head back to Jerusalem to search for him. They searched for three days until they found him in the temple. He is sitting with teachers, listening to them talk about God's Word and asking questions of them while at the same time amazing them with his understanding and answers about God's Word. His parents are frustrated with him, and he says, "Didn't you know that it was necessary for me to be in my Father's house?" Yet, Jesus obediently gets up and returns with them to Nazareth. Mary kept these things in her heart, and Jesus spent years growing in wisdom and stature and in favor with God and with people.

Throughout this story, there is an emphasis on the fulfillment of prophecy. This is no surprise when you consider the genealogy. While filled with many names, some more recognizable than others, it reveals a deep and powerful truth. God had worked through generations, bringing about the arrival of Jesus. He had connected people, given children to mothers, and heirs to fathers so that Jesus would come through Abraham, David, and many others. God was in control of bringing salvation to the world. The life of Jesus proves that God was making things happen.

TIMELINE OF THE LIFE OF JESUS

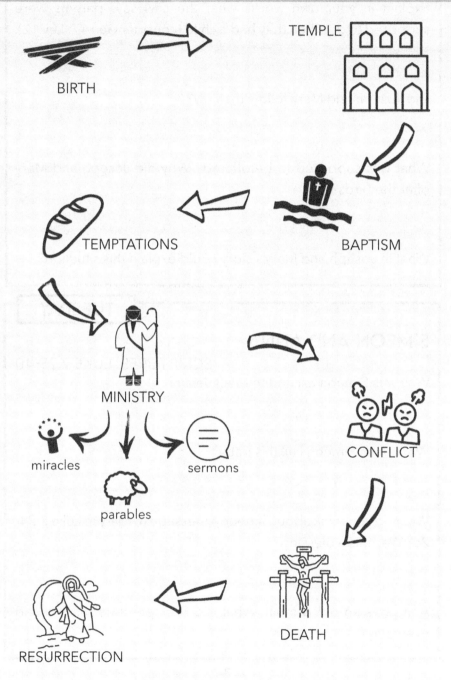

DEDICATION IN THE TEMPLE

SCRIPTURES: LUKE 2.21-24

Explain in your own words what the Law says parents were supposed to do when they had a child (consider Gen 17; Lev 12).

Did Joseph and Mary follow the Law?

What was supposed to be offered? Why did Joseph and Mary offer the birds?

What in Joseph and Mary's story could explain this situation?

SIMEON AND ANNA

SCRIPTURES: LUKE 2.25-40

Why was Simeon excited to meet Jesus?

What does Simeon call this baby?

What do you think about Simeon's message to Mary in Luke 2.24-25? Was this a blessing?

Anna was an old woman. What did she spend her time doing every day?

THE WISE MEN

SCRIPTURES: MATTHEW 2.1-12

How many wise men were there? Check your answer in the Bible.

Where were the wise men from?

What gifts did they bring Jesus?

Why did they not return to Herod?

MASSACRE OF THE CHILDREN

SCRIPTURES: MATTHEW 2.13-23

Why was Herod angry?

He required the killing of what?

This fulfilled a prophecy of Jeremiah. What did the prophet say?

Where did Joseph and Mary go to escape the danger?

JESUS IN THE TEMPLE

SCRIPTURES: LUKE 2.41-50

What was Joseph and Mary's yearly custom?

When Jesus went missing, where was he?

What was his response to his parents when they asked him why he had disappeared?

What does the Bible say about Joseph and Mary when Jesus gave them this response?

GENEALOGY

SCRIPTURES: LUKE 3.23-38

Name the people you recognize in Jesus's genealogy.

How far back does this genealogy go?

Matthew's genealogy mentions women. Does this one?

How many generations are mentioned in this genealogy?

DEEPER THINKING QUESTIONS

1 Why was it important for Jesus to be circumcised?

2 Joseph and Mary offered a pair of doves. What in their story could explain why this was necessary for them?

3 Simeon prophesied a gloomy message to Mary. When was this fulfilled?

4 What can we learn from the example of Anna?

5 These wise men are never said to be Jews. What can we learn from this?

6 Why did they give Jesus gold? Frankincense? Myrrh?

7 They followed a star to find Jesus. They were given a direct message from God about not returning to Herod. What can we learn about how God gives messages from their experience?

8 Joseph and Mary escape to Egypt. When else in the Bible have people escaped danger by going to Egypt?

9 Joseph and Mary came back from Egypt once Herod died. Yet they still avoided Herod's territory and settled in Galilee (Nazareth). Why?

10 When Jesus was 12, he would have possibly been considered accountable to the Law. This is the year he remains in the temple. What does this teach us about our own accountability?

11 How did Joseph and Mary feel when they lost Jesus?

12 Jesus's response is sometimes thought to be rude. What do you think?

13 Jesus goes home with his parents and it says that he "grew in wisdom and stature and increased in favor." What does this mean?

14 Name three differences between the genealogy of Luke and the one of Matthew.

NOTES

A voice came from heaven: "You are my beloved Son; with you I am well-pleased."
Luke 3.22b

WEEK 3
BAPTISM

IMMERSION & TEMPTATION

Complete Reading:
Matthew 8; Mark 2-3; Luke 5-7

Years have passed in the story of Jesus. Many conjecture that Jesus would have grown up as a typical firstborn son, with the same expectations that any firstborn son would experience. This includes caring for his family if anything bad happened, which many think did as we never read about Joseph after the story of Jesus's childhood. If Joseph had died, and Jesus was the firstborn son among several siblings, Jesus would be responsible for taking care of His family and providing for them. This could explain why He waits until 30 years old before He begins His ministry. Another reason for Jesus to wait until He was 30 is that Jews did not consider men capable of leadership until that age. Despite the many Jewish leaders in their history who were younger, some of their greatest led at 30 (Joseph, David, etc.).[1]

The gospels tell us that Jesus was baptized around this time. John, the cousin of Jesus, started a ministry that included baptism. He is teaching repentance and baptizing respondents in the Jordan River. It seems many were coming to him to be baptized, realizing their problem of sin and need for forgiveness. The Jewish leaders are disturbed about this itinerant preacher who is baptizing people, so they send some spies and eventually come themselves to question John. They ask if he is the Messiah, and he admits that he is not, but that he is the forerunner of the Messiah who was still to come. John does not identify the Messiah as Jesus.

> Baptism is the catalyst to spiritual maturity, not the sign of having attained it.
> -J.D. Greer

---

1   The Mishna Bruna also identifies 30 as the "prime of life" when a man is finally humble and broken enough to offer sincere prayer (O.C. 581:1).

Matthew, Mark, and Luke tell the story of Jesus going to John. John argues that Jesus should baptize him, but Jesus says that He must do it to "fulfill all righteousness." John baptizes Jesus, and the heavens open up. The Spirit comes down to Jesus in the form of a dove, and the Father speaks comforting words: "This is my beloved Son, with whom I am well-pleased." This affirmative statement is surely a great comfort.

Jesus is whisked away to the wilderness as soon as the baptism finishes. The gospels record one of those encounters for us near the end of Jesus's fast. We have few details about the fast, and the Jews had many fasts for various reasons. It seems Jesus was undergoing a long fast and was committed to doing so.

The devil shows up and actively tries to tempt Jesus in various ways. The devil is ultimately trying to create doubt in Jesus. While we do not know what the devil knows or is ignorant of, we do know that he knows Jesus is something special. It is hard to believe the devil is unaware of Jesus's identity, considering the things he tries to convince Jesus to do.

The first temptation in both Matthew and Luke's stories is for Jesus to turn the rocks into bread. You can imagine that this is a thought that has already been in Jesus's mind, as hungry as he was and as much as stones would look like loaves of bread. Yet, Jesus refused to break his fast to do a miracle that only benefitted Him. Instead, he quoted scripture to the devil. "Man must not live on bread alone but on every word that comes from the mouth of God."[2]

The devil then moves to temptations two and three, which are flip-flopped in the gospel accounts. Matthew says the devil took Jesus to the pinnacle of the temple and tempted him to throw himself off. While this does not sound tempting, the reason would. The devil quoted Psalm 91.11-12, which states that the one sent by God would not be injured but protected by God. Jesus refuses to give into the temptation and states, "Do not test the Lord your God."[3]

The third temptation (according to Matthew) is the devil taking Jesus to a high mountain top and showing him the kingdoms of the world. The devil

---

2   Jesus quotes Deuteronomy 8.3.
3   Jesus quotes Deuteronomy 6.16.

offers to give all of those kingdoms to Jesus if he bows down and worships him. Jesus says, "Go away, Satan! For it is written: Worship the Lord your God, and serve only him."[4]

All three times, Jesus refuses to give in to temptation. Yet, what we learn here is that Jesus did face temptations. Jesus was human, like you and me. There were things that He wanted but could not have. He had to tell himself no. He had to think critically about decisions, about each outcome, and decide what was the best outcome. Jesus struggled with having too little, with doubts and sorrows, and faced life the same way you and I do.

The devil, if anything, was more focused on causing the failure of Jesus than he is on any of us, yet we find in other passages that Jesus is said to have never sinned (cf. John 7.18; 2 Cor 5.21; Heb 4.15; 1 Pet 2.22). He did not lie, steal, murder, or commit adultery. He also did not gossip, slander, give into lust, or betray others. Jesus was not only a Redeemer (which we will see in lesson 10), but He was an example. As a human, he succeeded where we all fail (cf. Rom 3.23).

This also means that He, among all humans who ever lived, is the only one who did not deserve death (cf. Rom 6.23). He is the only one who avoided the cause of death. His life is the perfect example of how we should live. This is why studying and dwelling on the life of Jesus is so important. He tells us and shows us exactly how we should be living. As God says at the baptism of Jesus, he says later, "This is my beloved Son, with whom I am well-pleased." But note what God adds in this later story—"Listen to him!"

---

4   Jesus quotes Deuteronomy 6.13.

BAPTISM IN THE NEW TESTAMENT

John baptizes many in the Jordan	"for repentance"	
Jesus by John	"to fulfill all righteousness"	
3,000 on Pentecost	"for forgiveness of sin" to "receive the gift of the Holy Spirit" (2.38)	Acts 2
At Solomon's Porch	"so that your sins may be wiped out" (3.19)	Acts 3-5
Simon of Samaria	"in the name of the Lord Jesus" (8.16)	Acts 8
Ethiopian Treasurer	after learning about Jesus	Acts 8
Saul (Later Paul)	"wash away your sins, calling on the name of the Lord" (22.16)	Acts 9, 22, 26
Cornelius and his household	"in the name of Jesus" (10.48)	Acts 10
Lydia and her household	"to respond to what Paul was saying" (16.14)	Acts 16
Philippian Jailer and his household	"to be saved" (16.30)	Acts 16
The Corinthians	when they "believed" (18.8)	Acts 18
The Ephesians	in response to Jesus and to receive the Holy Spirit (19.2-4)	Acts 19

Now there is "one baptism" (Eph 4.5) "for the forgiveness of sins" and "the gift of the Holy Spirit" (Acts 2.38) that "saves you" (1 Pet 3.21).

BAPTISM OF JESUS (SYNOPTICS)
SCRIPTURES: MATT 3.13-17; MARK 1.9-11; LUKE 3.21-22

Where did Jesus go to be baptized? And by whom?

What did John argue with Jesus about?

Why did Jesus say that John should baptize Him?

What happened when Jesus came up from the water?

BAPTISM OF JESUS (JOHN)
SCRIPTURES: JOHN 1.19-34

Who is telling the story in this passage?

Who interrogated John? What did they ask?

What was John's answer to those asking his identity?

What does John call Jesus when he sees Him in the distance?

TEMPTATION—STONES TO BREAD

SCRIPTURES: MATT 4.1-4; LUKE 4.1-4

Who led Jesus into the wilderness to be tempted?

What was Jesus not doing while in the wilderness? For how long?

What did the devil ask Jesus to do that would have been tempting?

Why did Jesus not do it? Where is the passage Jesus quoted?

TEMPTATION—THROW DOWN FROM TEMPLE

SCRIPTURES: MATT 4.5-7; LUKE 4.9-12

Where did the devil take Jesus?

What did the devil ask Jesus to do?

Do you think the devil is properly quoting (or understanding) the Old Testament? Is the devil right?

Why did Jesus not do this? Where is the passage Jesus quoted?

TEMPTATION—KINGDOMS OF THE WORLD
SCRIPTURES: MATT 4.8-10; LUKE 4.5-8

Where did the devil take Jesus?

What did the devil ask Jesus to do?

Do you think the devil had the ability to give Jesus what he offered?

Why did Jesus not do this? Where is the passage Jesus quoted?

GOD'S COMFORT
SCRIPTURES: MATT 4.11; LUKE 4.13

How much did the devil tempt Jesus?

What happened to the devil when he failed to tempt Jesus to sin?

What did God do for Jesus once the temptations were over?

Where does Jesus go next?

DEEPER THINKING QUESTIONS

1 John the Baptizer was teaching "Repent, for the Kingdom of Heaven is at hand." What does repent mean?

2 What does "the Kingdom of Heaven is at hand" mean?

3 Why is Jesus baptized? What does this mean?

4 Is this the same reason others were baptized?

5 Why did John not want to baptize Jesus but wanted Jesus to baptize him instead? Are there any other passages in the Bible that explain this for us?

6 What is different between John's baptism and our baptism today?

7 Why was it important for John to know who the Messiah was?

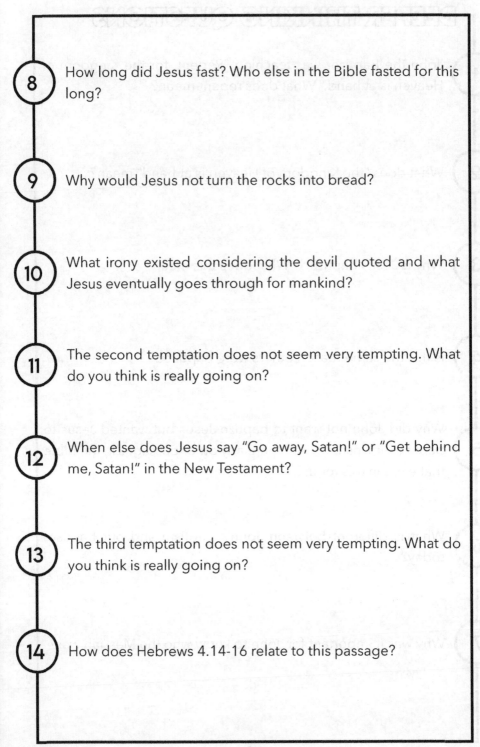

8 How long did Jesus fast? Who else in the Bible fasted for this long?

9 Why would Jesus not turn the rocks into bread?

10 What irony existed considering the devil quoted and what Jesus eventually goes through for mankind?

11 The second temptation does not seem very tempting. What do you think is really going on?

12 When else does Jesus say "Go away, Satan!" or "Get behind me, Satan!" in the New Testament?

13 The third temptation does not seem very tempting. What do you think is really going on?

14 How does Hebrews 4.14-16 relate to this passage?

NOTES

Now Jesus began to go all over Galilee, teaching in their synagogues, preaching the good news of the kingdom, and healing every disease and sickness among the people.
Matthew 4.23

SERMON

SERMON

Complete Reading:
Matthew 9-10; Mark 4-5; Luke 8-9

The first sermon recorded in the New Testament is a masterpiece of wisdom, admonition, and counter-cultural teachings. Often called the Sermon on the Mount (or the Sermon on the Plain when referring to Luke's version), it is also the longest single sermon recorded in the New Testament. Jesus's words are challenging and demand diligent searching to mine their depths.

The sermon itself is an exposé on the many ways the Jewish people had misunderstood the Old Testament law and how they had twisted it to their liking. This is why Jesus is upfront about not coming to abolish the Law. He did not want them to think He was trying to take anything away from God's command. Instead, He is helping them to realize that God's Law was not a checklist of dos and don'ts but a set of rules to reveal the character of God Himself. If they correctly understood the Law, it would reveal the nature of God's Kingdom as it had always been. We know Jesus's concern in His preaching is explaining the Kingdom they had not understood. "Now Jesus began to go all over Galilee, teaching in their synagogues, preaching the good news of the kingdom, and healing every disease and sickness among the people."[1]

When Jesus tells them the beatitudes, He shares that God's Kingdom does not work like earthly kingdoms. On earth, it is all about positions of power and reputations, displaying strength and military might, or stepping over and on people to get ahead. Contrarywise, the Kingdom of Heaven focuses on humility, submission, and mercy. As people develop the qualities of this Kingdom, God blesses them with His blessings. Likewise, Jesus shows that those in this Kingdom act differently. They are salt. They

---

[1]   Matthew 4.23

are lights that stand out in the darkness. When they do well, they bring attention to their King instead of themselves.

Jesus also helps them to reevaluate their understanding of the Law, which would have been glimpses into God's Kingdom. When the Law said, "Thou shalt not kill,"[2] it meant more than avoiding the extinguishing of life. He meant not to let killing be a part of our thought process. Avoid hating. Avoid slandering. Avoid name-calling. Avoid angering others for selfish benefit. When the Law said, "Thou shall not commit adultery,"[3] it meant to avoid even lusting after a woman. The Law said to divorce by giving a written notice,[4] but Jesus said that God intended marriage for life except in extreme circumstances. When the Law said to "not break your oath," [5]it meant they were to avoid making oaths at all because we are not in control—the King is. None of these erased past commands but explained them again by focusing on their true intention.

> "The Sermon on the Mount cannot be a merely human production. This belief enters into the very depth of my conscience. The whole history of man proves it."
> -Daniel Webster

He goes further in this sermon by helping them see the hypocrisy they practiced in their worship and devotion. They gave alms, but they did it for attention. They prayed in public, but they did it so others would admire them. They fasted on a regular schedule but made a show of it. Jesus tells them all of this is wrong. What we do for God, we do only for God. Therefore, He encouraged these hypocrites to give privately, to pray in a closet, and to make sure they looked great when they fasted so none would know what they were doing. What we do for God only benefits us when we do it for attention because such besmirched worship is worthless to God.

Jesus also spends a significant amount of time talking about how to eliminate worry in our lives. First, we must ensure that we are not living for

---

2   Exodus 20.13
3   Exodus 20.14
4   Deuteronomy 24.1
5   Leviticus 19.12

money, resources, or convenience. Instead, we live for God. If we put God first, He will take care of the rest. He will provide for our food and clothing. He will make sure we have enough to do well. Our society says that all of this depends on us, which is stress-producing. Jesus says to put all of that in the hands of God, which reduces stress. Instead, Jesus teaches us to put our eyes on God and trust Him for our belongings. He will provide for us if we will work for Him.

There is so much in this sermon that helps us to focus on the things of God's Kingdom, which is not of this world. It is different. It requires us to live differently if we are going to belong to this King. We won't sit around judging others unfairly. We will trust our King to give us the things we need, which are spiritual in nature. This God is generous and gives abundantly. We will take the "narrow path" where few walk. We will do the less common things to walk through the narrow door.

Many will think they are on this path, but they are not. They think they have earned their spot in God's Kingdom because they do great deeds on God's behalf, but because they are doing these things to get attention (considering the context of chapter 6 and the fact that they are bragging about their good deeds to God), God does not see their works. God does not know how they are. God rejects them from the Kingdom.

We must learn that being in God's Kingdom requires us to submit ourselves to the King, live how He wants us to, and live for His good pleasure. When we do, we will find that His good pleasure is to give for our good. He gives food and clothing, but more importantly, He gives forgiveness and salvation.

THE COUNTERCULTURAL SERMON OF JESUS

The Beatitudes:

"poor in spirit" = "I am nothing"

"meek" = "I care what's best for you"

"mourn" = "I am sorry"

"hunger and thirst for righteousness" = "I care about what is right"

"merciful"= "I forgive you"

"pure in heart" = "I care about what God wants"

"peacemakers" = "I will be anyone's friend"

"suffer persecution" = "I will do what is necessary, no matter what."

"love your enemies and pray for those who persecute you"

"if anyone slaps you on your right cheek, turn the other to him also."

"seek first the kingdom of God and his righteousness,"

"go into your private room, shut your door, and pray."

"whatever you want others to do for you, do also the same for them,"

store up for yourselves treasures in heaven,

The Blessings:

"...the kingdom of heaven is theirs."

"...they will be comforted."

"...they will inherit the earth."

"...they will be filled."

"...they will be shown mercy."

"...they will see God."

"...they will be called sons of God."

"...the kingdom of heaven is theirs."

THE BEATITUDES

SCRIPTURES: MATT 5.1-12; LUKE 5.20-26

List the beatitudes below and what is gained from each:

Blessed are the _____ for they _____

Blessed are the _____ for they _____ .

Blessed are the _____ for they _____ .

Blessed are the _____ for they _____ .

Blessed are the _____ for they _____ .

Blessed are the _____ for they _____ .

Blessed are the _____ for they _____ .

Blessed are the _____ for they _____ .

What differences exist between Matthew's list and Luke's list?

HATRED, HONESTY, & HONOR

SCRIPTURES: MATT 5.13-37

Why does Jesus compare us to salt? What about light?

Christ did not come to abolish the Law. What did He do instead? What does this mean?

What two of the Ten Commandments does Jesus talk about starting in verses 21? What does Jesus teach about them?

LOVE

SCRIPTURES: MATT 5.38-48; LUKE 6.27-36

What instruction shocks you most in Matt 5.38-42?

How should we treat our enemies?

How does God treat His enemies?

What are we if we treat our enemies as God treats His enemies?

PRAYER, FASTING, AND FORGIVENESS

SCRIPTURES: MATT 6.1-34

What do the hypocrites do when they give? What should we do?

What do the hypocrites do when they pray? What should we do instead?

What do the hypocrites do when they fast? What should we do instead?

Write out the model prayer found in 6.9-13.

JUDGING OTHERS

SCRIPTURES: MATT 7.1-12; LUKE 6.37-42

How can we avoid being hypocrites?

Does this mean we should never judge others? Explain your answer.

If we ask, seek, or knock, what will happen? What does this mean?

Write out the command in 7.12 that we call "the golden rule."

FALSE PROPHETS AND FALSE CONFIDENCE

SCRIPTURES: MATT 7.13-27; LUKE 6.43-49

What is the difference between the two ways talked about in Matt 7.12-13?

Describe the false prophets.

What can a good tree not do? What can a bad tree not do?

Describe the people who thought they were right with God but are not. What does Jesus say to them?

DEEPER THINKING QUESTIONS

1 Which of the beatitudes in Matthew 5.3-10 is most startling to you. Explain.

2 What lessons can we learn from being compared to salt?

3 What lessons can we learn from being compared to light?

4 What does Matthew 5.22 mean?

5 How serious does God consider our relationship with our brethren? What are we to put aside to repair relationships?

6 Why does Jesus tell us not to swear oaths?

7 How long are we to "turn the other cheek?"

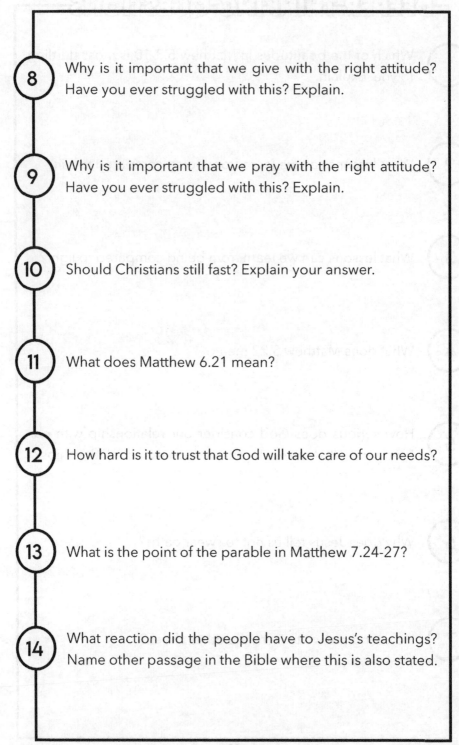

8 Why is it important that we give with the right attitude? Have you ever struggled with this? Explain.

9 Why is it important that we pray with the right attitude? Have you ever struggled with this? Explain.

10 Should Christians still fast? Explain your answer.

11 What does Matthew 6.21 mean?

12 How hard is it to trust that God will take care of our needs?

13 What is the point of the parable in Matthew 7.24-27?

14 What reaction did the people have to Jesus's teachings? Name other passage in the Bible where this is also stated.

NOTES

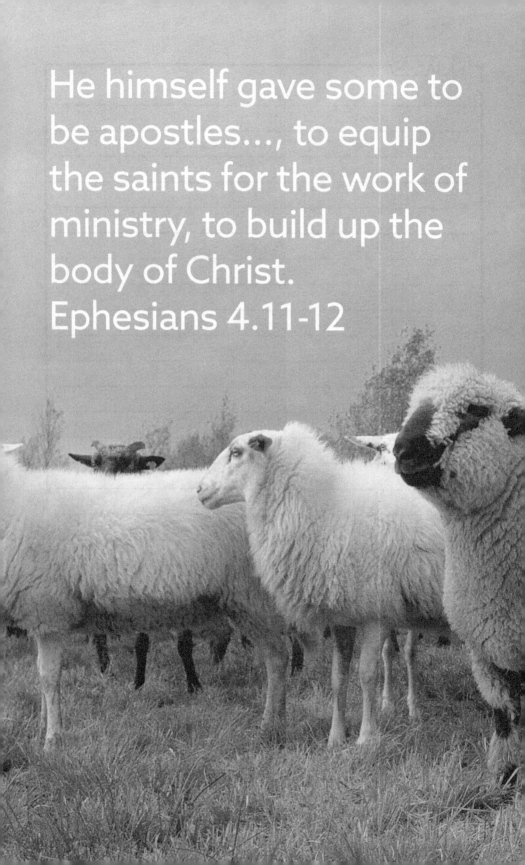

He himself gave some to be apostles..., to equip the saints for the work of ministry, to build up the body of Christ.
Ephesians 4.11-12

WEEK 5

DISCIPLES

DISCIPLES

A disciple is a follower and refers to anyone loyal to someone or something. In the New Testament, it is someone faithful to Jesus. There were many disciples in the gospel stories, both men and women, primarily Jews, but even a few Gentiles showed deference to Jesus.

An apostle is something different. They are a disciple because they are loyal to Jesus but also have a special purpose. The Greek word means "called out" or "set apart" for a special purpose. They were chosen and given a special job. That job is identified in Acts 1 when they determine to choose a new apostle to take Judas's place (he committed suicide after betraying Jesus). When verbalizing the criteria for someone becoming an apostle, they include three criteria:

1. Accompanied the group while Jesus interacted with them.

2. Was there from the baptism of John.

3. Until the death, burial, resurrection, and ascension.

These three criteria mattered because the apostles' primary mission was to be eyewitnesses, especially of the resurrection.[1] The apostles, especially by the time of the early church, were the local experts on Jesus, including His character, teachings, and the truth of His resurrection.

As apostles, they had special access to Jesus during His earthly ministry. they traveled with Him, watched His miracles, heard His teachings, and were able to have special audiences and ask Him questions others could not. They celebrated Passover with Him, and a few of them even saw the transfiguration. As John later says,

> What was from the beginning, what we have heard, what we have seen with our eyes, what we have observed and have touched with our hands,

---

1   This whole story is found in Acts 1.13-22.

concerning the word of life— that life was revealed, and we have seen it and we testify and declare to you the eternal life that was with the Father and was revealed to us— what we have seen and heard we also declare to you, so that you may also have fellowship with us; and indeed our fellowship is with the Father and with his Son, Jesus Christ.[2]

Notice John's claim to knowledge and authority: He has seen, heard, and even touched with his own hands. He knows what he is talking about when he talks about Jesus. He is an eyewitness. He has experienced Him. He knows His Savior both as a Redeemer and friend.

Most of the apostles were ordinary men. They were not specially trained by theologians or scribes. They were not of high social standing or wealthy. They were not politically powerful or of royal descent. Peter, Andrew, James, and John were fishermen.[3] They seemed to have their own business, nets, and boats and worked this job with their father. It is also possible that Thomas, Nathaniel, and Philip might also have been fishermen due to their fishing after the resurrection.[4] The only other apostle whose job we know is Matthew, who was a tax collector.[5]

> We esteem, honor, and love the apostles more than the other saints, because they served God more faithfully and because they loved Him more perfectly.
> -Ignatius

We also know that there would have been reason for conflict among the apostles. Simon is called a Zealot, known for their passion for overthrowing the Roman government.[6] He would have struggled with Matthew's past as a tax collector, a job that collected money for the Roman government. It seems James and John are called "sons of thunder," which likely refers to their attitudes and personalities.[7]

Regardless of the potential for division, Jesus united them to help the Messiah reach the world. They came together in harmony because

2   1 John 1.1-3
3   Matthew 4.18-22
4   John 21.2-8
5   Matthew 9.9
6   Matthew 10.4; Mark 3.18; Luke 6.15; Acts 1.13
7   Mark 3.17

they were disciples of the Prince of Peace.

We do not know why Jesus specifically chose these twelve men. Among them was Judas, a dishonest man who stole from their money bag and eventually betrayed Jesus to the Jewish authorities. None of the apostles were perfect men. They made mistakes and sometimes spoke foolishly. Peter argued with Jesus. Thomas asked a lot of questions. James was apparently quite young. Yet, before Jesus chose these men, he prayed all night in preparation for this great decision. [8]

These men would change the world. As witnesses to the greatest events in history, they would eventually be said to "turn the world upside down."[9] With the help of God and the power of the Holy Spirit, they convinced people all over the world that Jesus was the Messiah, the Redeemer of mankind.

It did not take powerful and highly educated men to make a difference—it took servants—those willing to follow Jesus, who led them to the despair of the cross and the victory of the resurrection.

---

8   Luke 6.12
9   Acts 17.6

THE DEVOTION OF THE TWELVE APOSTLES

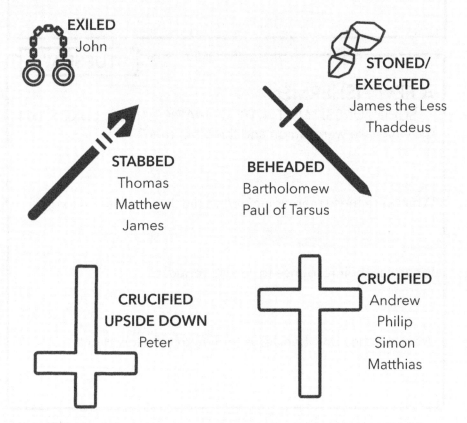

EXILED
John

STONED/ EXECUTED
James the Less
Thaddeus

STABBED
Thomas
Matthew
James

BEHEADED
Bartholomew
Paul of Tarsus

CRUCIFIED UPSIDE DOWN
Peter

CRUCIFIED
Andrew
Philip
Simon
Matthias

THE FIRST CHOSEN

SCRIPTURES: JOHN 1.35-51

Who was the first disciple of Jesus? Who did he tell about the Messiah?

What did Jesus tell Philip to do?

Who did Philip tell about Jesus? What did this man say?

Why did he start to believe that Jesus was the Messiah?

A FEW FISHERMEN

SCRIPTURES: MATT 4.18-22; MARK 1.16-20; LUKE 5.1-11

On what lake were Simon and the other men?

What were these men doing? What did Jesus ask them to do?

What was their response to Jesus's request?

What did they do when Jesus told them to follow Him?

THE TWELVE APOSTLES

SCRIPTURES: MATT 10.1-4; MARK 3.13-19; LUKE 6.12-16

Write down the list of the apostles in the order they are in each list:

THE WOMEN WHO FOLLOW JESUS

SCRIPTURES: LUKE 8.1-3

How are the women described who follow Jesus?

How were these women helping out the ministry of Jesus?

What other passages mention the women who follow Jesus?

SENDING OUT THE TWELVE

SCRIPTURES: MATT 10.1-31; MARK 6.6-13; LUKE 9.1-6

When Jesus sent out the Twelve, what did He give them the ability to do?

What were they told not to do?

What were they told to do?

What were they to do if they were rejected by a city?

SENDING OUT THE DISCIPLES

SCRIPTURES: LUKE 10.1-24

How did Jesus send out the seventy-two disciples?

Why was He sending them out? What was their job?

What abilities did He give them?

What was the response of the seventy-two at the end of their mission?

DEEPER THINKING QUESTIONS

1 What can we learn about sharing Jesus with others from Andrew?

2 Why did Nathaniel have a low opinion of Nazareth?

3 What lessons can we learn from the types of men Jesus chose as disciples?

4 When Jesus called the fishermen, what did they do? What does this teach us?

5 Is there any pattern to the lists of the apostles?

6 Jesus had many women who followed him. Name some women who have played major roles in Scripture.

7 Why do you think no women were chosen to be apostles?

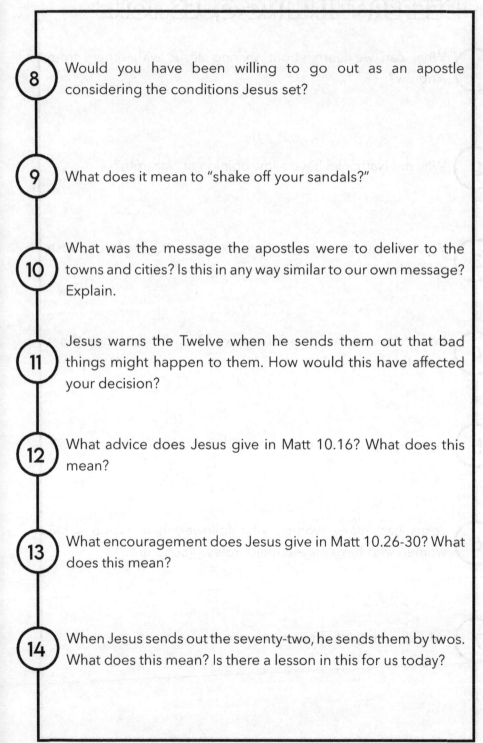

8 Would you have been willing to go out as an apostle considering the conditions Jesus set?

9 What does it mean to "shake off your sandals?"

10 What was the message the apostles were to deliver to the towns and cities? Is this in any way similar to our own message? Explain.

11 Jesus warns the Twelve when he sends them out that bad things might happen to them. How would this have affected your decision?

12 What advice does Jesus give in Matt 10.16? What does this mean?

13 What encouragement does Jesus give in Matt 10.26-30? What does this mean?

14 When Jesus sends out the seventy-two, he sends them by twos. What does this mean? Is there a lesson in this for us today?

NOTES

The blind receive their sight, the lame walk, those with leprosy are cleansed, the deaf hear, the dead are raised, and the poor are told the good news, and blessed is the one who isn't offended by me."
Matthew 11.5-6

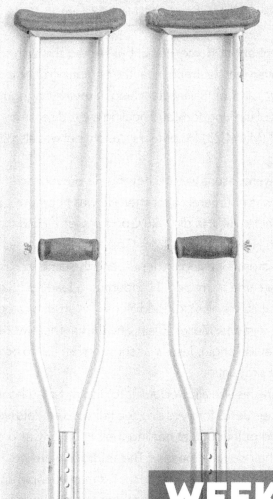

WEEK 6

MINISTRY

MINISTRY

Jesus went about doing good, but He did this with purpose. Matthew makes an overview statement near the beginning of his gospel. "Now Jesus began to go all over Galilee, teaching in their synagogues, preaching the good news of the kingdom, and healing every disease and sickness among the people" (Matt 4.23). He primarily taught but was also known for miracles and healing.

Miracles were Jesus's way of showing His provenance. He was not merely a man. He was not merely a teacher. He was not merely a worker of good deeds. What He did, He did with God's power. If He did miracles by God's power, then His words were from God also. When Jesus walked on water, calmed the storms, healed the lepers and the lame, or cast out demons, He showed He came from God. Nicodemus, a leading Pharisee, recognized the truth of this. [1] He also grouped Himself in an elite category of those who performed miracles: Moses, Elijah, and Elisha. These were all prophets and heroes of Jewish origin. Jesus was showing Himself to be equally from God as were the prophets.

These miracles also allowed Jesus to display His authority to do the works of God. When Jesus forgives sins, the religious leaders would get upset, so Jesus would point out that healing their infirmity was proof that He could also heal their spiritual needs. [2] The miracles were not intended to be a fixing of earthly problems. If so, Jesus left many people unhealed and failed in His mission. Rather, the miracles were to help Jesus fix the real problem we face—a problem of sin.

To that end, Jesus spent most of His time teaching instead of merely doing

---

1   John 3.2
2   Luke 5.17-39

miraculous deeds. He showed special concern in explaining the Kingdom of God. Many of His parables focused on this topic, explaining the nature of the Kingdom and the importance of its impact. He told parables that used everyday objects and people to explain confounding spiritual ideas. The parable of the sower sowing seed, the lost sheep, the mustard seed, or the wedding feast all revealed some truth about the nature of the Kingdom. Ultimately, as you gather the evidence of what Jesus was teaching, He wanted His listeners to know that God is King, His Kingdom was present and real, and that those who wanted to know God must submit themselves to His rule. This was not self-serving because God is love and cares for us. Jesus revealed that God was not a needy king wanting servants but a compassionate King who wanted to care for His people.

To prove this point, Jesus also taught how far God was willing to go to care for these people. He talked historically about God, who cared for the Israelite nation, and He revealed that God would continue to protect and provide for the world in the future through the work of the Son of God, Jesus Himself. Jesus would end up revealing that He had two purposes on earth.

First, He came to reveal the Father.[3] Jesus's actions and character displayed His Father's actions and character. Jesus spoke God's words. Jesus humanized God in a way that called humans to live like God. This is reflected in

"A man who was merely a man and said the sort of things Jesus said would not be a great moral teacher. He would either be a lunatic — on the level with the man who says he is a poached egg — or else he would be the Devil of Hell. You must make your choice. Either this man was, and is, the Son of God, or else a madman or something worse. You can shut him up for a fool, you can spit at him and kill him as a demon or you can fall at his feet and call him Lord and God, but let us not come with any patronizing nonsense about his being a great human teacher. He has not left that open to us. He did not intend to."- C.S. Lewis, *Mere Christianity*

teachings like "love your enemies,"[4] "take up your cross and follow me,"[5] and "turn the other cheek."[6] Jesus did not mind thwarting expectations and calling His followers to live separately and differently from the world.

Second, Jesus came with a mission to save. "For the Son of Man has come to seek and to save the lost."[7] Sometimes, he calls the Jews "the lost sheep of Israel."[8] At other times, He speaks of the lost of the world, including the Gentiles. Jesus would confront the Jews regarding their traditions because they had allowed their ideas about God's Word to become more important than God's actual Words. He would heal on the Sabbath. He would teach against their oath-making. He would point out their inconsistencies. In many of His teachings and stories, He exalted Samaritans and Gentiles [9](who the Jews hated) as the heroes and made the Jews the wicked. These confrontational teachings eventually led Jesus into conflict, yet this conflict ultimately accomplished His task of being the sacrifice needed to eliminate the guilt of sin.

Among His disciples, Jesus spent less time in conflict and more time teaching the character of Kingdom citizens. He taught humility and exemplified it through washing feet.[10] He taught productive purpose and displayed His point by cursing a fig tree.[11] He taught sacrificial service and demonstrated it on the cross.

4   Luke 6.27-28
5   Matthew 16.24
6   Matthew 5.39
7   Luke 19.10
8   Matthew 15.24
9   Matthew 8.5-13; Luke 7.1-10
10   John 13.1-17
11   Matthew 11.12-25

THE 40 PARABLES OF JESUS

Jesus, over the course of a three year ministry, became known as a great teacher and storyteller. He would often tell stories, known as parables. We have 40 recorded for us in Scripture. Many of these stories were told to reveal the characteritics of the Kingdom of Heaven. These are each worth studying and learning more from Jesus what we can know about God as our King.

Counting the Cost	Pharisee & Tax Collector
Dragnet	Place of Honor
Fig Tree	Returning Owner
Friend Seeking Bread	Rich Fool
Good Samaritan	Rich Man & Lazarus
Great Banquet	Sheep and Goats
Growing Seed	Shrewd Manager
Treasure and Pearl	Sower
Homeowner	Talents
Lamp Stand	Ten Virgins
Leaven	Tenants
Lost (Prodigal) Son	Two Sons
Lost Coin	Unfruitful Fig Tree
Lost Sheep	Unmerciful Servant
Master & Servant	Watchful Servants
Moneylender	Wedding Banquet
Mustard Seed	Weeds
Narrow Door	Wise & Foolish Builders
The New Cloth & Wineskin	Wise & Foolish Servants
Persistent Widow	Workers in the Vineyard

** For a more detailed study, check our the Daily Bread Teen Bible Study series book on the Parables of Jesus.

CALMING THE STORM

SCRIPTURES: MATT 8.23-27; MARK 4.35-41; LUKE 8.22-25

Why were Jesus and His disciples in the boat?

What tragic event started? What was Jesus doing during the tragic event?

What did Jesus say to the disciples after he fixed the problem?

What did the disciples say about Jesus?

FEEDING THE 5,000

 SCRIPTURES: MATT 14.13-21; MARK 6.30-44; LUKE 9.10-17

Why are the people hungry? What does Jesus find with which to feed the people?

What does Jesus have the apostles do to the people? What happened?

This is one of the only stories found in all four gospels (it is also in John 6.1-15). Why do you think all four writers thought this story was so important?

COST OF FOLLOWING JESUS

SCRIPTURES: MATT 8.18-22; LUKE 9.57-62; 14.25-35

What does Jesus say about our relationship with our families? What does this mean?

What does Jesus say we must bear if we are going to follow Him? What does this mean?

Jesus uses two illustrations to show the foolishness of not planning ahead. What are they? What is He teaching in your own words?

JESUS PREACHES FROM ISAIAH

SCRIPTURES: LUKE 4.16-30

Jesus read from Isaiah. What passage did He read from?

When He rolled it up, what did He announce to the people?

What was their response? What did they understand Him to be teaching?

What did Jesus say about His hometown?

THE FOUNDATION OF THE CHURCH
SCRIPTURES: MATT 16.13-20; MARK 8.27-30; LUKE 9.18-21

What did Jesus ask His disciples? What was their response?

What did Peter say?

What did Jesus say about Peter's confession?

What did Jesus say about the Church?

FORGIVENESS
SCRIPTURES: MATT 18.15-22; LUKE 17.3-4

If your brother sins against you, what should you do?

If he does not pay attention to you or others, what should the Church do?

How many times should you forgive your brother?

Jesus follows this by telling a parable. Retell the story in your own words:

DEEPER THINKING QUESTIONS

1   Why was Jesus able to sleep in the boat during the storm?

2   When Jesus fed the 5,000, what did they take up at the end? Why do you think this was an important detail to mention?

3   How many miracles are included in all four gospels? List them here.

4   Jesus did some amazing miracles. Write down several that amaze you the most.

5   Obviously Jesus did much more preaching than we had space to talk about in this lesson. What teachings stand out to you the most?

6   What does it mean to "count the cost?" How does this relate to your faith?

7   Jesus quoted Isaiah and then applied it to Himself. What was Jesus teaching?

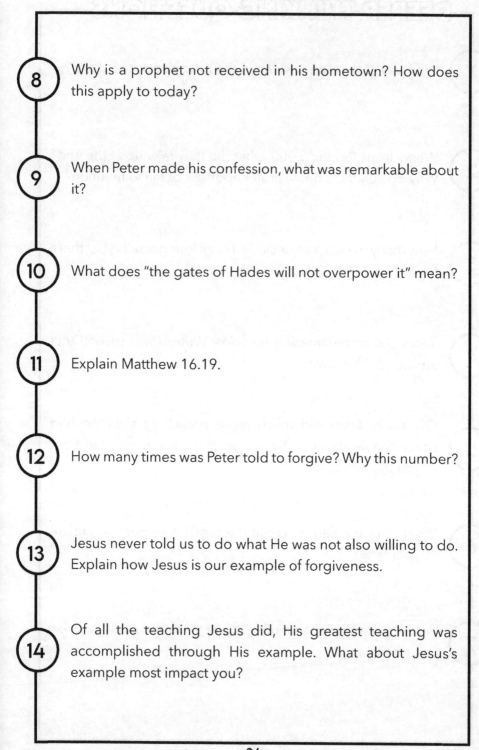

8 Why is a prophet not received in his hometown? How does this apply to today?

9 When Peter made his confession, what was remarkable about it?

10 What does "the gates of Hades will not overpower it" mean?

11 Explain Matthew 16.19.

12 How many times was Peter told to forgive? Why this number?

13 Jesus never told us to do what He was not also willing to do. Explain how Jesus is our example of forgiveness.

14 Of all the teaching Jesus did, His greatest teaching was accomplished through His example. What about Jesus's example most impact you?

NOTES

Children, it is the last
hour, and as you have
heard that antichrist is
coming, so now many
antichrists have come.
Therefore we know that it
is the last hour.
1 John 2.18

WEEK 7
ENEMIES

ENEMIES

Complete Reading:
Matthew 15-17; Mark 10; Luke 14-15

As impressive as the ministry of Jesus was, filled with teaching of kindness, mercy, forgiveness, and love, He suffered at the hands of many throughout His work. Early in His ministry, His hometown rejected Him. He taught the Scriptures with a clear application about Himself, and they rejected Him. The audience on that occasion was so angry that they drove Him out of town to the edge of a cliff with the intention of hurling Him over the edge.[1] He did a great miracle in a Gentile town, casting out a demon from a possessed man, and because some pigs were killed, they asked Him to leave.[2] No matter where Jesus went, some wanted Him gone.

The enemies of Jesus can be categorized into several groups. Right at the beginning of Jesus's life, Herod made himself an enemy of Jesus. When the wise men came seeking the newborn king, Herod tried to trick them into revealing Jesus's location. When they did not, Herod attempted to kill Jesus by killing the young boys in the town of Bethlehem. He hoped to kill anyone who might usurp the throne from him. His actions caused Joseph and Mary to carry Jesus to Egypt for the rest of his reign, and when they returned to Israel, they settled in Nazareth.

Then, before Jesus's ministry began, we are introduced to the Sadducees and Pharisees who come questioning John's authority to baptize the people. John recognizes their intentions and calls them a "brood of vipers."[3] These two groups would be problems for the entirety of Jesus's work.

The Pharisees were the sect of Jews that became the most prevalent contrarians. Some think their name comes from the Hebrew word prushim,

---

1   Luke 4.16-30
2   Matthew 8.28-34
3   Matthew 3.7

meaning "separated ones." Their sect emerged around 150 years before Jesus arrived, and they were known for righteousness, law-keeping, and piety. It would be great if they were not also known for hypocrisy and for doing what they did to be seen by men. They constantly sent spies to see Jesus's teachings, moles to try and trap Him, and they would question Him often. They were deeply concerned about blasphemy and losing their power in the communities. Scribes were frequently Pharisees and were the local experts on the Law. These two groups are often mentioned together in the gospels. The thing that often set the Pharisees on edge was any argument with the oral tradition of the rabbis. They were concerned not just with keeping the Sabbath but also with maintaining the traditions of the Sabbath. They considered a violation of tradition on par with violating the Law of God. This led to multiple conflicts with Jesus and was often the basis for their accusations against Him. Yet, in order to see this group fairly, we must recognize that what they were seeking to do was good. They cared about purity and righteousness. They loved the truth. Some were even recognized as good men (like Nicodemus[4]). Pharisees were good people who had allowed themselves to focus on the wrong things.

> "Jesus Christ lived in the midst of his enemies. At the end all his disciples deserted him. On the Cross he was utterly alone, surrounded by evildoers and mockers. For this cause he had come, to bring peace to the enemies of God. So the Christian, too, belongs not in the seclusion of a cloistered life but in the thick of foes. There is his commission, his work."
> -Deitrich Bonhoeffer

Sadducees were another sect of Judaism, dramatically different than the Pharisees. They often were politically powerful and motivated. They were responsible for maintaining the Temple by the time of Jesus, and many served on the Sanhedrin, the Jewish governing body in Jerusalem. They were also often the priests who served in the Temple and thereby had much influence

---

4   First mentioned in John 3.1-13. He is identified as a follower of Jesus in John 19.39.

among the people. They disagreed with the Pharisees on the role of tradition, believing only the written Torah had God's authority. They did not believe in an afterlife or supernatural beings like angels or spirits. This led to dissension between them and the Pharisees and an entirely different worldview. Pharisees lived this life in preparation for the next life. Sadducees lived this life for what they could enjoy. Pharisees were much more willing to be poor for the sake of riches in the afterlife. The Sadducees wanted to be rich in this life. Despite their differences, they were united in their feelings towards the teachings and ministry of Jesus.

The Pharisees and the Sadducees tried to confront Him near the end of His ministry, and Jesus handily won the debates.[5] They often tried to trap him into teaching what was unpopular (to diminish His popularity with the people) or teaching what was blasphemous (so they would have a reason to execute Him). Jesus always won the debates.

Even among Jesus's followers, there were enemies. Several times, Jesus they tried to kill Jesus.[6] Other times, entire crowds walked away from Jesus. Judas is famous for his betrayal of Jesus.[7] In the end, all of the apostles deserted Him. Jesus's work was polarizing, at the least, and led to many enemies.

---

5   Matthew 22
6   Besides the occasion early in His ministry, they also tried to stone Him in John 8.59.
7   John 6.60-66

AROUND 4 MILLION JEWS

JEWISH PEOPLE & THEIR SECTS

PHARISEES:

Around 6,000 during the time of Jesus, representing around 1.5% of the population. They focused on law-keeping and tradition. Often the scribes were Pharisees.

ESSENES:

Around 4,000 or 1% during the time of Jesus, though not mentioned in the Bible. They were a separated community that focused on Bible learning and the coming Messiah.

SADDUCEES:

A small percentage and much smaller than other sects. These did not believe in a resurrection and only in the Torah. They were wealthy, kept the temple, and were friendly with Rome.

JESUS REJECTED IN HIS HOMETOWN
SCRIPTURES: MATT 13.53-58; MARK 6.1-6; LUKE 4.16-30

Where is Jesus's hometown?

What Scripture did Jesus read in His hometown? What did He teach about that passage?

What was the reaction of the people initially?

What did Jesus do few of in this town?

REJECTED BY PIG FARMERS
SCRIPTURES: MATT 8:28-34; MARK 5.1-20; LUKE 8.26-39

Describe the man who is healed in this story.

What did the demons say to Jesus? What did Jesus allow? What happened to these animals?

What was the reaction of the towns people?

What was the reaction of the healed man?

PHARISEES TRY TO TRICK JESUS

SCRIPTURES: MATT 22.15-22

Why did the Pharisees ask Jesus a question?

What was the question?

How did Jesus answer the question?

SADDUCEES TRY TO TRICK JESUS

SCRIPTURES: MATT 22.23-33

Why did the Sadducees ask Jesus a question?

What was the question?

How did Jesus answer the question?

A LAWYER TRIES BUT JESUS WINS

SCRIPTURES: MATT 22.34-46

Why did the lawyer ask Jesus a question?

What was the question?

How did Jesus answer the question?

What question did Jesus ask them?

JESUS PRONOUNCES WOES

SCRIPTURES: MATT 23.1-39

List the woes below.

1 What does Jesus mean when He says a prophet has no honor in His hometown?

2 What made the people in His hometown so angry that they wanted to kill Him?

3 When healed the man among the tombstones, what do we expect the reaction to be? What is it instead?

4 Why do you think the reaction was so negative?

5 Do you think there is any connection between the meaning behind Pharisee ("separated ones") and the meaning behind the Greek word for church ("those called out")? Explain.

6 Name several places in the gospels where Jesus had conflict with the Pharisees.

7 What story does Jesus tell at the beginning of Matthew 22 that sets the stage for the conflict with the Pharisees and Sadducees?

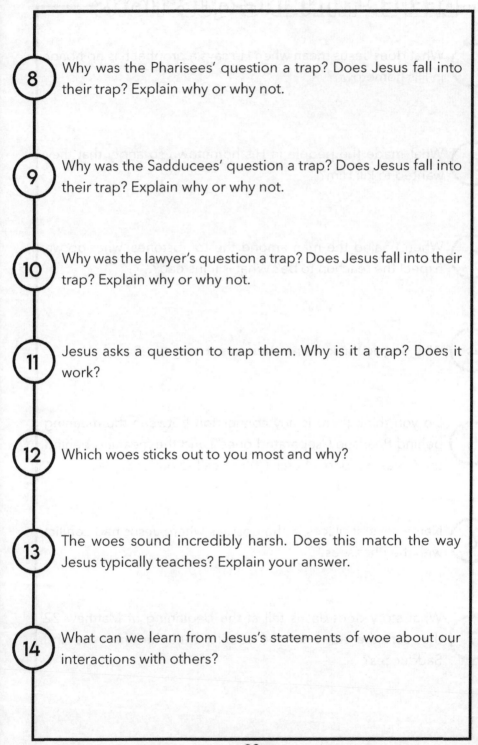

8 Why was the Pharisees' question a trap? Does Jesus fall into their trap? Explain why or why not.

9 Why was the Sadducees' question a trap? Does Jesus fall into their trap? Explain why or why not.

10 Why was the lawyer's question a trap? Does Jesus fall into their trap? Explain why or why not.

11 Jesus asks a question to trap them. Why is it a trap? Does it work?

12 Which woes sticks out to you most and why?

13 The woes sound incredibly harsh. Does this match the way Jesus typically teaches? Explain your answer.

14 What can we learn from Jesus's statements of woe about our interactions with others?

NOTES

When the time came to completion, God sent his Son, born of a woman, born under the law, to redeem those under the law, so that we might receive adoption as sons.
Galatians 4.4-5

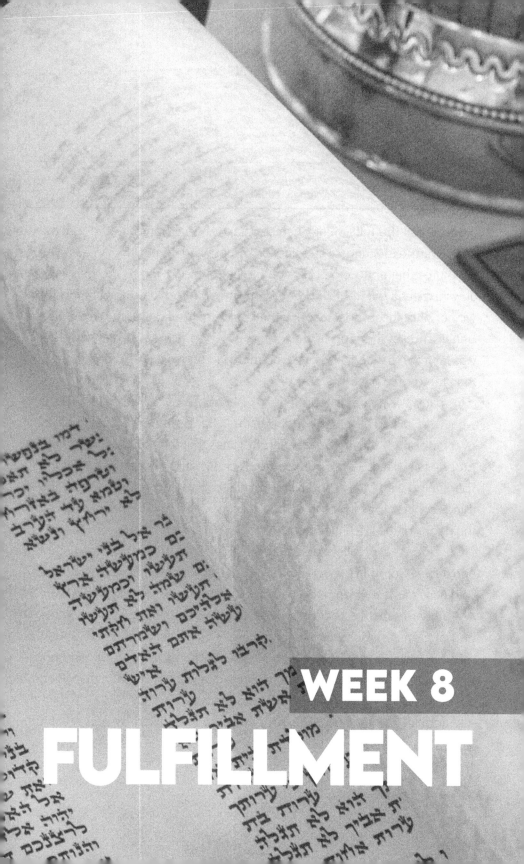

WEEK 8

FULFILLMENT

FULFILLMENT

Complete Reading:
Matthew 18-20; Luke 16-18

Jesus was the fulfillment of an expectant hope. Ironically, though, the Jews were expecting something or someone different than Jesus. The scriptures that announced His coming were misinterpreted to make the Jews expect a different kind of Savior. They wanted a triumphant King, a winner of battles, and a leader who would charge against Rome on their behalf and set them up as the victorious world power. Jesus's Kingdom was far from that concept, but even more victorious over a bigger enemy than they could have imagined.

In many ways, they should have expected a savior like Jesus. This is what was talked about throughout the Old Testament. Jesus fulfilled every prophecy they had, including the ones that they did not know were prophecies. Jesus spoke with some disciples after His resurrection, and "beginning with Moses and all the Prophets, he interpreted for them the things concerning himself in all the Scriptures."[1] Jesus is found throughout the pages of the Old Testament.

Consider the parallels between major heroes of the Old Testament and Jesus. Compare Jesus with Adam, the first created Son of God. Paul calls Jesus a "last Adam."[2] Jesus is similar to Isaac, especially in the story of Abraham's sacrifice of Isaac.[3] Jesus parallels the story of Joseph at the end of Genesis. Moses and Jesus share many traits, both in life and in mission. Jesus is like Joshua, with whom He shares a name. On and on, the characters in the Old Testament reveal glimpses of Jesus so that when Jesus arrives, He would seem familiar to them.

In addition, so many specific prophecies were fulfilled by Jesus that it

---

1   Luke 24.27
2   1 Corinthians 15.45-58
3   Genesis 22

should have been obvious to anyone paying attention that Jesus was the long-awaited Messiah. This became the teaching tool of the early Church, who "reasoned with them from the Scriptures, explaining and proving that it was necessary for the Messiah to suffer and rise from the dead: 'This Jesus I am proclaiming to you is the Messiah.'"[4] Jesus was the Messiah, and it can be proven with reasonable evidence.

Consider the earliest prophecy on record, all the way from God's mouth in the Garden of Eden. After Adam and Eve sinned, God delivered consequences for their actions, including these words to the snake who deceived Eve. "I will put hostility between you and the woman, and between your offspring and her offspring. He will strike your head, and you will strike his heel."[5] This verse, often called the *protoevangelicum*, is the first glimpse of the good news made possible by Jesus. Abraham was promised that his obedience would bring blessings to the whole world.[6] In every generation that passed, God would become increasingly specific about who the coming Messiah would be.

"Christianity is the story of how the rightful king has landed, you might say landed in disguise, and is calling us to take part in a great compaign of sabotage."
-C.S. Lewis,
Mere Christianity

Of Noah's sons, Shem was chosen. Of Abraham's sons, Isaac was chosen. Of Isaac's, Jacob was chosen. Of Jacob's twelve sons, Judah was chosen. Each generation would expand the amount of people on earth, yet with each generation, God would narrow down the options for who would become the Savior. Judah was told that "the scepter would not part"[7] from his lineage, giving a kingly reference to the future. Moses was told that a new prophet like him would eventually come after him.[8] David is told that his descendant would sit on the throne forever.[9] It is easy

---

4   Acts 17.2-3
5   Genesis 3.15
6   Genesis 12.3
7   Genesis 49.10
8   Deuteronomy 18.15
9   2 Samuel 7.12-13

to see why the Jews were expecting a Savior. He was promised that this Messiah would be king.

Yet, the specific prophecies dealing with the circumstances of Jesus's life should have also revealed details that the Jews ignored. There would be a virgin birth.[10] The child would be born in Bethlehem.[11] His ministry would begin in Galilee.[12] The Messiah would teach in parables.[13] He would become the perfect sacrifice.[14] As the sacrifice, Jesus had to live a sinless life.[15] Eventually, the Messiah would be despised and rejected,[16] betrayed for 30 silver pieces,[17] hung on a cross,[18] and resurrected.[19]

When it's all added up, Jesus fulfilled, according to conservative estimates, over 300 prophecies. Many specific. Many obvious. Many outside of His control. Those who did not accept Jesus as the Messiah had to choose not to see the answer God was putting in front of them, and they did not want to see it because Jesus was the the kind of Messiah they wanted. Jesus spoke peace, while they wanted war. Yet, Jesus is the great Messiah, the hope of Israel, and the salvation of the entire world.

---

10   Issaiah 7.14; Luke 1.35
11   Micah 5.2; Matthew 2.4-6
12   Isaiah 9.1-2; Matthew 4.12-17
13   Psalm 78.1-2; Matthew 13.34-35
14   Psalm 40.6-8; Hebrews 10.5-10
15   Exodus 12.5; Hebrews 9.14
16   Isaiah 53.3; Luke 4.28-29
17   Zechariah 11.12-13; Matthew 27.6-10
18   Psalm 22.16; John 19.36-37
19   Psalm 16.9-11; Acts 2.31

THE 40 MIRACLES OF JESUS

Jesus turns water into wine at the wedding in Cana
Jesus heals nobleman's son at Capernaum in Galilee
Jesus drives out an evil spirit in Capernaum
Jesus heals peter's mother-in-law sick with fever
Jesus heals many sick and oppressed at evening
First miraculous catch of fish on sea of Galilee
Jesus cleanses the first leper
Jesus heals a paralytic let down from the roof
Jesus heals an invalid at Bethesda
Jesus heals a man's withered hand on the sabbath
Jesus heals a blind, mute demoniac
Jesus cleanses the second leper
Jesus heals centurion's palsied servant in Capernaum
Jesus raises a widow's son from the dead in Nain
Jesus calms a storm on the sea
Jesus casts demons into a herd of pigs
Jesus heals a woman with an issue of blood
Jesus raises Jairus' daughter back to life
Jesus heals two blind men
Jesus heals a man who was unable to speak
Jesus feeds 5000 men plus women and children
Jesus walks on water
Jesus heals many sick as they touch his garment
Jesus heals a woman's demon-possessed daughter
Jesus heals a deaf and dumb man
Jesus feeds 4,000 plus women and children
Jesus heals a blind man outside Bethsaida Julius
Jesus heals a boy with an unclean spirit
Miraculous temple tax in a fish's mouth
Jesus heals a mute demoniac
Jesus heals a woman crippled for 18 years
Jesus heals a man with dropsy on the sabbath
Jesus cleanses ten lepers on the way to Jerusalem
Jesus heals a man born blind by spitting in his eyes
Jesus raises Lazarus from the dead in Bethany
Jesus restores sight to Bartimaeus in Jericho
Jesus withers the fig tree on the road from Bethany
Jesus heals a servant's severed ear during his arrest
Resurrection of Jesus Christ
Second miraculous catch of fish at the sea of Galilee

JESUS AND ADAM

SCRIPTURES: ROM 5.12-21; 1 COR 15.45-58

What similarities exist between Jesus and Adam?

What contrasts exist between Jesus and Adam?

JESUS AND ISAAC

SCRIPTURES: GEN 22

What similarities exist between Jesus and Isaac?

What contrasts exist between Jesus and Isaac?

JESUS AND MOSES

SCRIPTURES: ACTS 7.17-36; HEB 11.23-29

What similarities exist between Jesus and Moses?

What contrasts exist between Jesus and Moses?

JESUS AND DAVID

SCRIPTURES: 1 SAM 16-17; ACTS 2.22-35

What similarities exist between Jesus and David?

What contrasts exist between Jesus and David?

FRIDAY

PROPHECIES

SCRIPTURES: ISA 53

What prophecies are in Isaiah 53 and where are they fulfilled in the New Testament?

SATURDAY

PROPHECIES

SCRIPTURES: PSA 22

What prophecies are in Psalm 22 and where are they fulfilled in the New Testament?

DEEPER THINKING QUESTIONS

1 Why were the Jews wanting a Savior during the first century?

2 What technologies and advancements made it convenient for Jesus to come at that time?

3 There are some similarities between Jesus and other cultural mythologies. How are these to be explained?

4 What similarities exist between Jesus and Moses?

5 What similarities exist between Jesus and Joshua?

6 What similarities exist between Jesus and Samson?

7 What similarities exist between Jesus and Elijah?

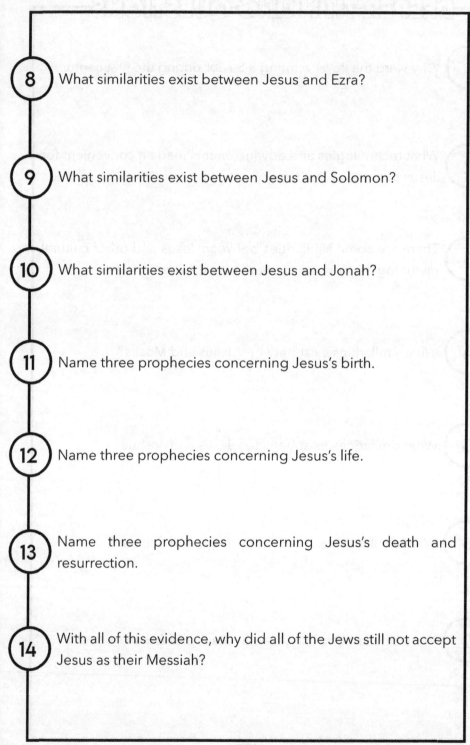

8 What similarities exist between Jesus and Ezra?

9 What similarities exist between Jesus and Solomon?

10 What similarities exist between Jesus and Jonah?

11 Name three prophecies concerning Jesus's birth.

12 Name three prophecies concerning Jesus's life.

13 Name three prophecies concerning Jesus's death and resurrection.

14 With all of this evidence, why did all of the Jews still not accept Jesus as their Messiah?

NOTES

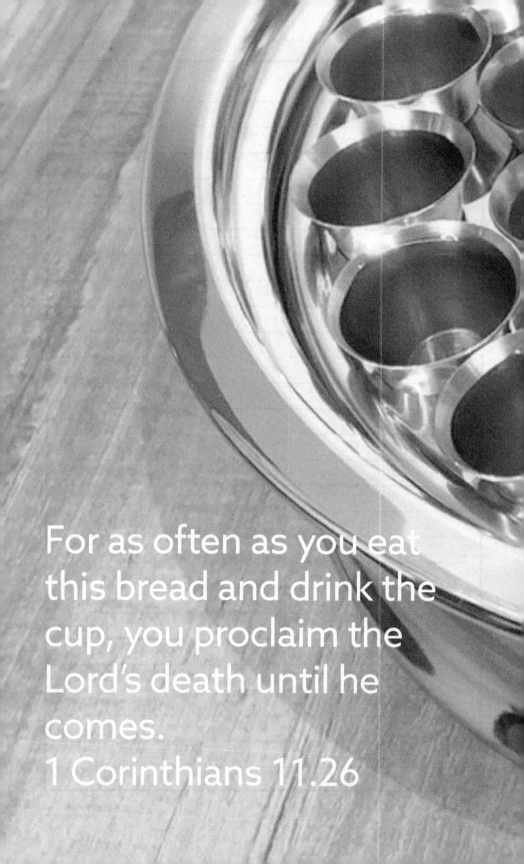

For as often as you eat this bread and drink the cup, you proclaim the Lord's death until he comes.
1 Corinthians 11.26

WEEK 9
COMMUNION

COMMUNION

Complete Reading:
Matthew 21-22; Mark 11-12; Luke 19-20

One of the most remarkable aspects of Jesus's ministry is His willingness to associate with anyone. This is also one of the reasons He made enemies. Jesus did not see people with a past but people with a future, and He wanted their future to be with Him. He ate with His disciples at a wedding feast where they witnessed Him turning water into wine.[1] He ate with tax collectors, a hated group of people who worked gathering taxes for the Roman government. [2]Multiple times, He ate with Pharisees who had invited Him into their homes.[3] He even ate with a leper whom we assumed was healed.

[4]On another occasion, he provided food for and ate with crowds of several thousand.[5] He ate grain with His disciples that they plucked from the grain in a field, which caused the Jews

"'Give us each day our daily bread' (Luke 11:2-3). That is how Jesus teaches us to pray. We need to pray for our daily bread not because we're worried about where our next meal might come from, but because we're not."

-Tim Chester, A Meal With Jesus

---

1   John 2.1-10
2   Matthew 9.9-17; Mark 2.13-22; Luke 5.27-39. He also went to Zacchaeus's house to eat with him in Luke 19.1-9.
3   At the house of Simon the Pharisee (Luke 7.36-50), with a "certain Pharisee" (Luke 11.37-54), and with one of the chief Pharisees (Luke 14.1-24).
4   John 12.1-11; Matthew 26.6-13; Mark 14.3-9. This might be the same occasion as Luke 7.36-50 considering the similarities of the story with Simon the Pharisee.
5   Jesus provided food for 5,000 men, along with women and children (Matthew 14.13-21; Mark 6.32-44; Luke 9.12-17; John 6.1-14) and for 4,000 on another occasion (Matthew 15.32-38; Mark 8.1-9).

to accuse them of the sin of working on the Sabbath.[6] Jesus was no stranger to eating with others in the field or at the table.

He also sat down and celebrated the Jewish feasts with His disciples, which is one of those occasions to which we turn our attention.[7] The time of the Passover arrives a meal that reminds the Jewish people of God's work, rescuing them from Egyptian slavery. When rescued, on the night when God sent the final plague that killed the firstborn of Egypt, God had them kill a lamb and use the blood to surround their doors to show they belonged to God. They were to eat unleavened bread because it would travel well, and they were to eat with a staff in their hand, ready to go.

Jesus and His disciples need a place to celebrate this meal together, so Jesus sends some disciples into town to look for a man who will open his house for them to eat together. They gathered in this upper room once it had been prepared, and Jesus ate the meal with them. The meal consisted of a plate of food with certain symbolic elements representing various aspects of the story of Israel's rescue from Egypt. Unleavened bread represented the bread they ate during their exodus. The lamb was a part of their Passover sacrifice. There were cups of wine that represented different aspects of the story and God's promises.[8]

While eating this meal with the disciples, Jesus repurposed several parts of the meal to represent a new rescue for God's people. He showed that the bread they broke and shared would represent His body, which would be broken for them. He showed that the wine they shared would represent His blood as it established a new covenant, like the blood of the bull, which was used to establish a new covenant with the people in Moses's time.[9] Jesus gave them this new meal as a new Passover, a new reminder of their covenant with their Savior. While the apostles would not yet understand what Jesus was doing, as He had not yet died, they

6   Matthew 12.1-8; Mark 2.23-28; Luke 6.1-5
7   Matthew 26.20-30; Mark 14.17-26; Luke 22.14-38; John 13.1-38
8   This story is found in Exodus 11-13, which explains the final plague, the rules of their meal, and the perpetuation of that meal for future generations that is called the Passover.
9   Exodus 24.3-8

understood and began this new meal called the Lord's Supper as soon as the church began.[10] This was not merely a memorial meal like the Passover, remembering a major historical event. This was a communion meal, where those who participated communed with each other and Jesus Himself. Paul calls it a "sharing in the blood" and "sharing in the body of Christ."[11] When we do this meal today, we are still sharing with Christ in communion, memorializing an eternity-changing event, and recommitting ourselves to the covenant we made by the blood of Jesus.[12]

Jesus ate several more meals with the twelve after this upper-room feast. Once was in the upper room where He explained His death and resurrection;[13] another was with some apostles by the seashore.[14] He also ate with two other disciples when He went with them to their house in Emmaus, revealing His resurrection so they would report it to the apostles.[15] Jesus was communion-focused, and today, we can also be due to the Lord's Supper. We can commune with a Savior who came to this earth to commune with His creation.

---

10   i.e., Acts 2.42
11   1 Corinthians 10.16
12   1 Corinthians 11.17-34
13   Luke 24.41-48
14   John 21.1-23
15   Luke 24.28-32

THE JEWISH PASSOVER

The Passover meal included six main elements, all significant to the story of the Passover. The lamb represented the sacrifice. The egg represented new life. The matzah, or unleavened bread, represented the haste with which they were to leave Egypt. Two bitter herbs represented the life of slavery they were leaving. The nuts and apples mixed represented the bricks they made in Egypt.

There were readings from the Scripture and recitations of the Exodus story and many traditions that surrounded the meal. It was a celebration of God's powerful deliverance and also included four important glasses of wine which correspond to God's promises in Exodus 6.6-7:

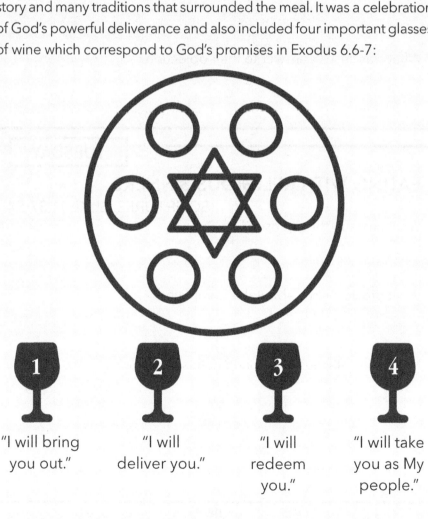

1 "I will bring you out."

2 "I will deliver you."

3 "I will redeem you."

4 "I will take you as My people."

EATING WITH SINNERS

SCRIPTURES: MATT 9.9-17; MARK 2.13-22; LUKE 5.27-39

What did Jesus tell Matthew to do? Did he do it?

While eating with Matthew, who else was at the meal?

Why did the Pharisees complain?

What was Jesus's answer to their objection?

EATING WITH RELIGIOUS SINNERS

SCRIPTURES: LUKE 11.37-54

What amazed the Pharisee?

What did Jesus say about this complaint?

Make a list of woes mentioned in this passage.

EATING WITH ANNOINTED FEET

SCRIPTURES: MATT 26.6-13; MARK 14.3-9; LUKE 7:36-50

Whose house did Jesus go to? Use all three passages to come up with your answer.

What happens to Jesus at this meal?

Who is the woman? Use all three passages to come up with your answer.

What was the disciples's response to this event?

LORD'S SUPPER IN MATTHEW

SCRIPTURES: MATT 26.17-30

How does Jesus send them to find a place to celebrate the Passover?

What distressing thing does Jesus announce at the Supper?

What does Judas ask? Why is this ironic?

What purpose does Jesus give for the bread?

FRIDAY

LORD'S SUPPER IN MARK

SCRIPTURES: MARK 14.17-26

What distressing thing does Jesus announce in Mark's account?

What purpose does Jesus give for the bread?

What purpose does Jesus give for the cup?

What did they do at the conclusion of the meal?

SATURDAY

LORD'S SUPPER IN LUKE

SCRIPTURES: LUKE 22.14-38

What distressing thing does Jesus announce at the beginning of the meal in Luke's account?

What purpose does Jesus give to the bread?

What purpose does Jesus give to the cup?

After the supper, what do the disciples argue about?

DEEPER THINKING QUESTIONS

1 Why do you think eating with others is so important in the New Testament and to Jesus?

2 Jesus's first miracle is at a wedding feast in John 2. Jesus's last interaction with the disciples is eating with them at the end of John's gospel. What does this tell us?

3 In our modern times, food is plentiful and accessible. Was that true back then? How would this change your understanding of Jesus making food (like when He fed the 5,000 or the 4,000)?

4 Jesus is called a "glutton and sinner" by His enemies (Matt 11.19). Why would they call Him this?

5 Jesus's disciples are condemned for not fasting (Mark 2.18-22). What was Jesus's answer?

6 The Lord's Supper is a regular part of modern day worship. What do you think about during this time of reflection?

7 Do you find the Lord's Supper meaningful? Explain your answer.

8 Jesus's conversation during the Lord's Supper would have been shocking to the disciples. Put yourselves in their shoes. What would have been shocking to you?

9 During the communion meal, several arguments happened. List them below.

10 Luke's account of the Lord's Supper does not follow the same pattern as Matthew and Mark. What is different about it?

11 Why do you think Luke includes this extra detail? Does this change our pattern?

12 Paul received instructions on the Lord's Supper from the Lord Himself. What instructions does Paul give on how to practice this memorial (see 1 Cor 11.23-26)?

13 What other purposes and thoughts did Paul instruct us to have at this Supper (see 1 Cor 11.17-32)?

14 How can your time during the Lord's Supper become more useful and focused?

NOTES

And he died for all so that those who live should no longer live for themselves, but for the one who died for them and was raised.
2 Corinthians 5.15

WEEK 10

DEATH

DEATH

Complete Reading:
Matthew 23-26; Mark 13; Luke 21

Jesus said, "For the Son of Man has come to seek and to save the lost."[1] He knew that people were lost in sin, that sin demanded death as a consequence,[2] and that sacrifices had long handled this. Yet, Jesus also knows that "it is impossible for the blood of bulls and goats to take away sins."[3] He knew that it would take the blood of a sinless man and that He was the only one qualified.[4]

Jesus went with His disciples to the Mount of Olives to a garden where He would often go to pray. Here, Judas came with a crowd and soldiers to arrest Jesus. He identified Him by kissing His cheek, and after a short scuffle, Jesus went with the guards as their prisoner. He was delivered to the house of Annas, the former high priest and unofficial leader of the Jewish people. He is condemned there for blasphemy and then taken to the official high priest named Caiaphas. Although Jesus made no defense, He is again condemned. He is then tried before a tribunal called the Sanhedrin, found guilty of blasphemy, and His sentence is execution. Throughout this mockery of a trial, the Jews broke dozens of their own laws so they could arrest and execute Jesus as a blasphemer.

They take Jesus to the house of Pilate, the Roman governor over Israel, and charge Him with treason. He finds no guilt in Jesus and sends Him to Herod, the Roman "king" over Israel, who also finds Him innocent, and Pilate tries to get Jesus out of punishment. He does not want to give the Jewish leaders what they want, and He does not want to execute Jesus, but because of pressure and threats from the Jewish

---

1   Luke 19.10
2   Genesis 2.16-17; Romans 6.23
3   Hebrews 4.10
4   2 Corinthians 5.21; Hebrews 4.15; 1 Peter 2.22; 1 John 3.5

leaders, Pilate delivers Jesus to them and authorizes His crucifixion.

Before we get to the crucifixion, consider what Jesus has already endured. He has not eaten and is forced to stay awake all night. He was immensely stressed in the garden as He prayed so that He sweat great drops of blood. He was beaten and abused during the Jewish trials. Bystanders whacked Him with reeds and hit him in the face. He was scourged, a horrible punishment that the Bible does not describe. Soldiers would take whips, often a "cat of nine tails," which had sharp shards of glass or pottery woven into the threads of the whip, along with weighted metal balls at the end, and tear off the flesh of a person's back. This scourging was designed to torture and cause damage. This would have effectively exposed the flesh and bone of His back, and they did this expertly to criminals to bring them close to death. Jesus had the skin ripped off again as they took the mocking robe from him. They put a crown of thorns on His head, which would have caused immense bleeding. He suffers incredibly before He ever makes it to Golgotha, the place of His crucifixion.

> "We are told that Christ was killed for us, that His death has washed out our sins, and that by dying He disabled death itself. That is the formula. That is Christianity. That is what has to be believed."
> -C.S. Lewis, *Mere Christianity*

Crucifixion was one of the most heinous and horrific ways to die. It was a punishment reserved for the worst of criminals or for unruly slaves. He was mocked and belittled. He was stripped naked, and his hands and feet were nailed to a wooden beam. He was then displayed to the world as He hung above them like a military trophy. The way they placed the body on the cross caused breathing to be labored, adding to the torture and making speaking difficult.

Yet, Jesus still found the strength to speak seven times from the cross:

1. "Father, forgive them; for they know not what they do."[5]
2. "To day shalt thou be with me in paradise."[6]

---

5   Luke 23.34
6   Luke 23.43

3. "Woman, behold, thy son! Behold, thy mother!"[7]
4. "My God, my God, why hast thou forsaken me?"[8]
5. "I thirst."[9]
6. "It is finished."[10]
7. "Father, into thy hands I commend my spirit."[11]

Each of these statements has significant meaning, being the words Jesus felt important enough to say through what we imagine would be gritted teeth and pain-filled groanings. So much more could be said about each statement and many other details from the crucifixion event, but the most crucial moment is when He died. He, who did not deserve death, died in our place. The God who created humanity became a man and died as a man so that we could live.[12] He became our sacrifice so that He could save us.

When He died, His body was removed from the cross, and Joseph of Arimathea and Nicodemus, a leading Pharisee, hurriedly put it in a tomb near Golgotha.

7   John 19.26-27
8   Matthew 27.46; Mark 15.34
9   John 19.28
10   John 19.30
11   Luke 23.46
12   Philippians 2.5-11

THE SEVEN STATEMENTS

1. **"Father, forgive them; for they know not what they do."**
   Jesus prays for the forgiveness of all those who are crucifying Him, from the soldiers, the Jewish leaders, and bystanders. He is concerned about their forgiveness from beginning to end.

2. **"Today shalt thou be with me in paradise."**
   Both theives who were cricified with Jesus rail insults and abuse, but one has a change of heart. He asks for Jesus's help and Jesus promises that he would see paradise.

3. **"Woman, behold, thy son! Behold, thy mother!"**
   Even from the cross, Jesus takes care of His earthly responsilbities.

4. **"My God, my God, why hast thou forsaken me?"**
   Jesus speaks this in Aramaic, and it seems to be a quote from Psalm 22, which teaches that God did not abandon Jesus.

5. **"I thirst."**
   Jesus was human with human needs. The exhaustion from the crucifixion causes Jesus to thirst and need help.

6. **"It is finished."**
   Jesus proclaims that His work if finally done. God's wrath is satisfied. Jesus knows the sacrifice for sin is complete.

7. **"Father, into thy hands I commend my spirit."**
   Jesus quotes from His beloved Scriptures to proclaim that He is doing the work of God, even through the agony of crucifixion.

THE ARREST
SCRIPTURES: MATT 26.36-56; MARK 14.32-52; LUKE 22.40-53
Where was this garden? Where is that in relation to Jerusalem?

What did Jesus pray in the gardem? How many times?

What did the apostles do while Jesus was praying?

Reading the different accounts, what happened when Jesus was arrested? What is most startling to you about this story?

THE JEWISH TRIALS
SCRIPTURES: MATT 26.57-27.2; MARK 14.55-15.1; LUKE 22.55-71
Jesus went three different places to stand trial before the Jews. Name them in order.

What is He accused of by the Jewish leadership?

What scripture does Jesus quote to the high priest? Why is this significant?

THE ROMAN TRIALS

SCRIPTURES: MATT 27.11-31; MARK 15.2-20; LUKE 23.1-25

Pilate was known as a scoundrel of a man. Does he seem this way in the Gospel accounts?

Why did Pilate not want to punish Jesus?

Name some of the evidence Pilate had of Jesus's innocence.

Pilate let Barabbas go instead. What do we know about Barabbas?

THE SCOURGING

SCRIPTURES: MATT 27.26; MARK 15.15; LUKE 23.22

What does the Bible tell us about scourging? Why?

Have you ever seen the scourging in a movie about Jesus?

Jews would whip someone 40 times maximum. The Romans had no limit to the amount of times they would whip someone. Which did Jesus receive?

Would you be willing to go through this for someone?

THE CRUCIFIXION

SCRIPTURES: MATT 27.31-56; MARK 15.20-41; LUKE 23.26-49

Crucifixion was horrific and designed to be excruciating. It was also designed to last a long time. How long did Jesus hang on the cross?

Name some supernatural things that happened while Jesus was on the cross.

After Jesus died, why did they have to break the legs of those crucified with Him?

JESUS'S DEATH AND BURIAL

SCRIPTURES: MATT 27.50-66; MARK 15.37-47; LUKE 23.46-56

It says Jesus gave up His spirit. What does this mean?

Who came to believe as a result of Jesus hanging on the cross?

What supernatural things happened when Jesus died?

Where did they lay the body of Jesus?

DEEPER THINKING QUESTIONS

1 What does Jesus pray for in the garden? What does He mean?

2 Why does Jesus pray for this three times?

3 When Judas comes for Jesus's arrest, what did Judas think would happen?

4 Jesus goes quietly with the guards. He is unjustly tried by the Jews. What does He say during these trials?

5 When Jesus appears before Pilate, name who comes to Jesus's defense.

6 What did Herod want to see when Jesus was sent to him?

7 When Pilate allowed Jesus to be crucified, what symbolic thing did he do to show he did not approve of this decision?

8 On the way to the crucifixion, what did they make Jesus do? Who did they force to help?

9 While Jesus was hanging on the cross, what did the sign say above His head?

10 When did it get dark during the crucifixion? What is the significance of this?

11 What were those crucified with Jesus guilty of? What were they doing during the crucifixion?

12 Name people who were at the crucifixion.

13 What happened when they pierced Jesus's side with the spear?

14 What is the significance of the temple veil being torn in two?

NOTES

We were buried therefore with him by baptism into death, in order that, just as Christ was raised from the dead by the glory of the Father, we too might walk in newness of life.
Romans 6.4

WEEK 11
RESURRECTION

RESURRECTION

Complete Reading:
Mark 14; Luke 22; John 13-16

The most crucial moment in the history of mankind is the resurrection of Jesus of Nazareth, the King of kings and Messiah of the Jews. This cannot be overstated or overemphasized. Indeed, essential moments led up to this moment, such as the creation, the giving of promises, and the birth of Jesus. Certainly, other vital moments made the resurrection possible, such as the death of Jesus on the cross. But the resurrection becomes the linchpin of our salvation, hope, and faith. Without it, we have nothing, and every other moment has no value. Paul stated as much in 1 Corinthians 15:

"If Jesus rose from the dead, then you have to accept all that he said; if he didn't rise from the dead, then why worry about any of what he said? The issue on which everything hangs is not whether or not you like his teaching but whether or not he rose from the dead."
- Timothy Keller, *The Reason for God: Belief in an Age of Skepticism*

Now I want to make clear for you, brothers and sisters, the gospel I preached to you, which you received, on which you have taken your stand, and by which you are being saved, if you hold to the message I preached to you–unless you believed in vain. For I passed on to you as most important what I also received: that Christ died for our sins according to the Scriptures, that he was buried, that he was raised on the third day according to the Scriptures,[1]

If Christ has not been raised, then our proclamation is in vain, and so is your faith.[2]

If Christ has not been raised, your faith is worthless; you are still in your sins.[3]

---

1   1 Corinthians 15.1-4
2   15.14
3   15.17

138

> If we have put our hope in Christ for this life only, we should be pitied more than anyone.[4]

We must believe in the resurrection and place our hope in it as Christians. It has to be the moment we know more than any other moment. Yet, this is sometimes hard because we also know that people do not come back from the dead on a semi-common basis. It is a miracle. It is not something we have seen nor will see until we all experience resurrection. This is the task the apostles were given by Jesus, which we will see in the next lesson. But to build our faith in this pivotal moment in history, let's consider a few reasons we should believe.

1. There were many witnesses. Paul makes a list of them. Cephas. The Twelve. Over five hundred brothers and sisters at one time. James. All the apostles. Paul also. In this incomplete list, Jesus appeared to the apostles who knew Him and believed in Him, James, his brother, who did not believe in Him, and an entire crowd. If someone wanted to verify this claim, they could ask Peter, Matthew, or one of that crowd. They could get evidence based on what those still alive had seen.

2. The first witnesses were women. This seems like a strange claim, but that's the point. In those days, the testimony did not come with any authority, yet they were the first to see Jesus. If the resurrection were fabricated and untrue, they would not have made the most important witnesses women. They would leave them off the list (as Paul did in 1 Corinthians). They would instead have created a more authoritative witness list.

3. The empty tomb. Peter makes this point in his sermon in Acts 2, but the tomb of Jesus remained empty. If Jesus had not been raised, the enemies and unbelievers could have produced the body and proved the resurrection wrong. They never did this, and it was never disproven.

4. The change in the witnesses. The apostles on the night of Jesus's crucifixion were nowhere to be found. They ran when He was arrested. Only John is mentioned at the cross. they cowered in the upper room

---

4   15.19

behind locked doors, thinking they would be next.[5] Yet, over the course of the next month, they went from hiding behind doors to preaching in the streets. They were willing to be arrested and even martyred for this claim that Jesus was raised from the dead. If this entire moment were artificial, why would these men and others be so willing to die for what they knew was a lie?

5. The lack of motivation for creating a lie. Not one group has a valid reason for lying about the resurrection. Jesus' enemies wanted him in the ground, and his friends were confused and lost. The apostles ended up dying for the claim, and it brought them nothing but persecution, poverty, and pain.

6. The change in history. This faith caught on, and it changed the world. The early church did not gain momentum because of carefully placed political candidates or because they threw a lot of money behind a marketing campaign. Instead, it grew because the people who believed sought to tell everyone they knew about what had happened. They sent people to the witnesses and proved with Scripture that this was God's plan all along.[6] This faith, despite the early persecution by both the Jews and the Romans, survived centuries of efforts to squash the movement.

There is more evidence of Jesus's resurrection from Christian and non-Christian sources than for any other historical event. This event is monumental for every person today, especially for Christians.

---

5   John 20.19
6   For instance, Acts 17.1-4

FIFTEEN PROOFS
OF THE RESURRECTION

1. The witness of women.

2. The empty tomb.

3. The guards.

4. The lack of motivations for deceit.

5. The appearances.

6. The inability of Jewish testimony to disprove.

7. The unlikely acceptance of a criminal sage.

8. The proximity of the claims to the event.

9. The transformation of cowards.

10. The conversion of Saul.

11. The growth of the Christian Church despite the work of the Jews.

12. The growth of the Christian Church in an antagonistic Roman world.

13. Sunday becoming a significant day of worship.

14. The parallel accounts to significant stories of other cultures - God uses the familiar to introduce the significant.

15. There are no other explanations.

Taken from Adam Shanks. *From Sunday to Sunday.* (Temple Terrace, FL: Florida College Press, 2024) 121-128. A more thorough examination is in those pages.

RESURRECTION IN MATTHEW

SCRIPTURES: MATT 28.1-15

What day of the week did Jesus rise from the dead?

What did the angel tell the women?

What did the women do?

What happened to the guards? What story was fabricated?

RESURRECTION IN MARK

SCRIPTURES: MARK 16.1-13

What worried the women as they came to the tomb?

What did they find when they arrived?

What did the young man dressed in a white robe tell them?

What did the women do?

RESURRECTION IN LUKE

SCRIPTURES: LUKE 24.1-12

Why were the women coming to the tomb?

What do they find? What are they told?

What women were there?

What did Peter see in the tomb?

RESURRECTION IN JOHN

SCRIPTURES: JOHN 20.1-18

What woman does John focus on in his account? What do we know about this woman?

Who does she see? Who does she think he is?

What does she call Jesus? What does this mean?

What does he tell her to do?

THE MEN ON THE ROAD TO EMMAUS

SCRIPTURES: LUKE 24.13-35

When the two disciples were walking home, what were they disputing about?

Who shows up and travels with them?

What does this stranger do while they walk home?

When they realize who this stranger was?

JESUS WITH HIS DISCIPLES AT THE SEA

SCRIPTURES: JOHN 21.1-23

Jesus finds the disciples doing what work?

What does Jesus tell them to do from the shore?

Why does this cause them to think this is Jesus?

What does Jesus ask Peter three times? What does Peter answer three times?

DEEPER THINKING QUESTIONS

1 Each resurrection account has many similarities. Write down 5 below.

2 Each resurrection account has some differences. Write some below.

3 How should we explain these differences?

4 How long was Jesus in the tomb? How long did he say He would be in the tomb?

5 Thinking back to the crucifixion accounts, what other amazing (miraculous) event happened the day of Jesus's resurrection?

6 Why were the apostles hiding in the upper room?

7 When Jesus appeared to the men on the road to Emmaus, how is He described?

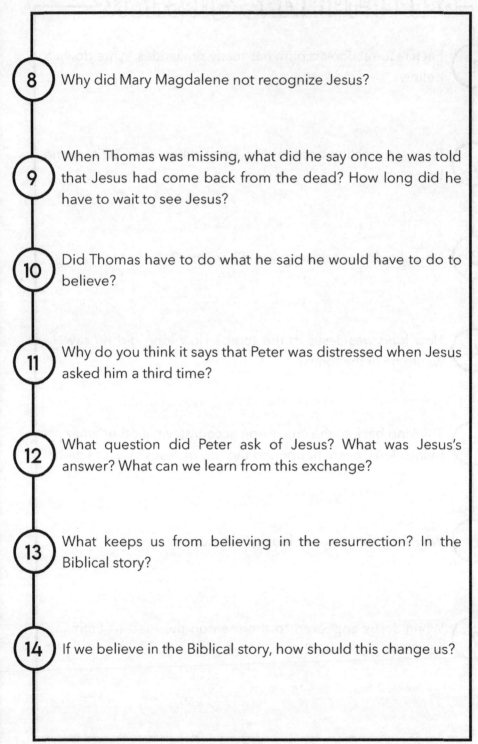

8 Why did Mary Magdalene not recognize Jesus?

9 When Thomas was missing, what did he say once he was told that Jesus had come back from the dead? How long did he have to wait to see Jesus?

10 Did Thomas have to do what he said he would have to do to believe?

11 Why do you think it says that Peter was distressed when Jesus asked him a third time?

12 What question did Peter ask of Jesus? What was Jesus's answer? What can we learn from this exchange?

13 What keeps us from believing in the resurrection? In the Biblical story?

14 If we believe in the Biblical story, how should this change us?

NOTES

For it says:
When he ascended
on high, he took the
captives captive; he gave
gifts to people. But what
does "he ascended"
mean except that he also
descended to the lower
parts of the earth? The one
who descended is also
the one who ascended far
above all the heavens, to fill
all things.
Ephesians 4.11-12

WEEK 12

ASCENSION

ASCENSION

Complete Reading:
Matthew 27-28; Mark 15-16; Luke 23-24

If any doubt existed in the apostles' minds, it was now erased. Jesus, whom they loved, was killed. They lost all hope. They lost all purpose. But just a few days later, they saw Him again. He had risen and restored all of the missing hope. Over the course of 40 days, He appeared to the apostles several times, rebuilding their faith and reminding them that this all had a purpose. He came to reveal the Father to us in a more real and tangible way, which He did through living His life perfectly and displaying the character of God in the way He lived.1 He came to seek and save the lost and made that possible through His sacrifice. 2He gave us hope of a future and a new Kingdom through the resurrection of a King.

Now, the purpose was expanding. Jesus gave what has come to be called "The Great Commission."3 They were to go about telling the world about Jesus, the Kingdom, and the invitation to become part of that Kingdom through being disciples, being baptized, and living for Him.

He also gave them the tools they needed to do this job. First, He opened their mind to understand the Scriptures.4 This was important because the apostles had shown unparalleled levels of misunderstanding as Jesus taught them. He had to unteach what their culture had told them so He could put in the right ideas. The Scriptures were the basis of their teaching, and the more they knew,

---

1   John 1.18
2   Luke 19.10
3   Matthew 28.19-20; Mark 16.15-16; luke 24.44-49
4   Luke 24.45

the more successful they would be. He also "breathed on them,"5 which gave them the Holy Spirit. This was not the miraculous gifts of the Holy Spirit they would receive in Acts 2, but it seems to be more associated with the Holy Spirit they offer everyone in Acts 2.38.

Once Jesus prepared these men for their work, He left. Instead of disappearing and leaving them with the possibility that He might show back up as He did multiple times during the forty days after His resurrection, He left in a spectacular way. He floated away. While ascending into the sky, angels appeared and told the apostles that Jesus would one day return the same way He went away. He would come on the clouds.6 When He comes again, it will be because it is over. Jesus is coming back one day to retrieve His own. He comes back to proclaim "game over," or "pencils down," and to take us to judgment.

Put yourself in an apostle's shoes. They've traveled with Jesus for three years. They have listened to Him teach, watched miracles, and participated in discussions about morality, responsibility, and the nature of the Kingdom. They have watched Jesus exemplify morality, responsibility, mercy, kindness, and love. They have traveled around the countryside and through city centers with the teacher. They have watched others abuse him, despise Him for no reason, and experience hate by those who should have loved Him best. They have been witnesses to the major moments of Jesus's life, from His baptism with water to His baptism of persecution. They have felt the pain of losing Him, felt the overflowing joy of realizing He resurrected, and then felt the loss of Him ascending. A few of them watched Him transfigure on the mountaintop, and now they have watched Him ascend to the place where He really belongs. They sat with Him in boats, fished with Him,

> "The whole of history since the ascension of Jesus into heaven is concerned with one work only: the building and perfecting of this 'City of God.'"
> — Saint Augustine

---

5   John 20.22
6   1 Thessalonians 4.13-18

and joked around with Him. He was their friend and colleague. He was their leader, their teacher, and their superior. He was their hope, and now He was gone. They watched Him leave in the splendor of the ascension, but the end result was loneliness.

Yet, the apostles did not end there. They changed their lives. They devoted themselves to the spreading of the Gospel message and the building of the Kingdom. They went from uneducated fishermen to confounding apologists who shared the message of the King. They became ambassadors.[7] They do the work that Jesus gave them to do. They started in Jerusalem, defeating the arguments the Jewish leadership made against their movement, entirely dedicated to talking about Jesus to anyone who would listen. They then spread to Samaria and the surrounding areas. Eventually, over the course of a few decades, they took the Gospel to every known part of the world.

Some backwoods, country, uneducated fishermen who were hilariously hopeless students, often buffoons in the presence of Jesus's teachings, became the teachers to the world. They found their purpose in the simple job of telling people what they had witnessed. John says it best in His writings:

> What was from the beginning, what we have heard, what we have seen with our eyes, what we have observed and have touched with our hands, concerning the word of life—that life was revealed, and we have seen it and we testify and declare to you the eternal life that was with the Father and was revealed to us—what we have seen and heard we also declare to you, so that you may also have fellowship with us; and indeed our fellowship is with the Father and with his Son, Jesus Christ. We are writing these things so that our joy may be complete.[8]

7   2 Corinthians 5.20
8   1 John 1.1-4

MESSIANIC PROPHECIES
THE DEATH AND RESURRECTION OF JESUS

	OUR PASSOVER LAMB	
"It is the Lord's Passover" (Exodus 12.21-27).		"For Christ our Passover lamb has been sacrificed" (1 Corinthians 5.7).
"You may not break any of its bones" (Exodus 12.46).	**NO BROKEN BONES**	"They did not break his legs since they saw that he was already dead" (John 19.31-36).
"Moses made a bronze snake and mounted it on a pole. Whenever someone was bitten, and he looked at the bronze snake, he recovered" (Numbers 21.9).	**LIFTED UP TO BE SEEN**	"Just as Moses lifted up the snake in the wilderness, so the Son of Man must be lifted up." (John 3.14).
"My God, my God, why have you abandoned me?... Everyone who sees me mocks me; they sneer and shake their heads..." (Psalm 22.1, 7).	**FORSAKEN & SCORNED**	"Those who passed by were yelling insults at him,... the chief priests, with the scribes and elders, mocked him..." (Matt 27.39, 41).
"They pierced my hands and my feet" (Psalm 22.16). "They will look at me whom they pierced" (Zechariah 12.10).	**PIERCED HANDS AND FEET**	Also, another Scripture says: They will look at the one they pierced" (John 19.36-37).
"For you will not abandon me to Sheol; you will not allow your faithful one to see decay" (Psalm 16.10).	**WOULD NOT SEE DECAY**	He spoke concerning the resurrection of the Messiah: He was not abandoned in Hades, and his flesh did not experience decay" (Acts 2.31).
"I know that my Redeemer lives..." (Job 19.23-27).	**RISE AGAIN**	"An hour is coming, and is now here, when the dead will hear the voice of the Son of God, and those who hear will live" (John 5.24-29).

THE GREAT COMMISSION
SCRIPTURES: MATT 28.16-20; MARK 16.13-18; LUKE 24.36-49

What is the great commission?

Does this still apply to us today?

How can we accomplish this work?

THE ASCENSION
SCRIPTURES: MARK 16.19-20; LUKE 24.50-52

Put yourself in the apostles' shoes. How would this moment make you feel?

It seems they stood staring at the sky long after Jesus was no longer seen. What do you think they were hoping for?

What does the angel tell them?

What did they do?

THE BREATH OF JESUS

SCRIPTURES: JOHN 20.19-23

Jesus breathed on them and told them to, "Receive the Holy Spirit." Why is this significant?

When else has God breathed on men?

How important is the Holy Spirit in the coming work of the apostles?

UNBELIEVERS BELIEVE

SCRIPTURES: JOHN 20.24-29

Thomas does not believe Jesus has resurrected when Jesus first appeared because Thomas did not get to see Him. What did Thomas say He would need to do in order to believe?

When Jesus appeared, did Thomas do what he said he would do?

What did Thomas say? What did Jesus say about those who do not get to see?

THE EXALTATION OF JESUS

SCRIPTURES: PHI 2.5-11

This poem in Philippians tells the amazing story of Jesus. List the many ways Jesus humbles Himself.

List the ways God exalts Jesus.

THE GLORIFIED JESUS

SCRIPTURES: REV 1.9-20; 19.11-16

When Jesus has returned to glory, how is He described in these two passages in Revelation? Make a list below.

DEEPER THINKING QUESTIONS

1 What would be your feelings if you were a disciple who witnessed the arrest and trials of your Lord Jesus? Explain.

2 What would be your feelings if you were a disciple who witnessed the crucifixion of your Lord Jesus? Explain.

3 What would be your feelings if you were a disciple who witnessed the resurrection of your Lord Jesus? Explain.

4 What would be your feelings if you were a disciple who witnessed the ascension of your Lord Jesus? Explain.

5 Explain the Great Commission in your own words.

6 Did the apostles obey this commission? Explain.

7 Do we obey this commission? Explain.

8 Jesus equipped the apostles for this work. Does He equip us for the work? Explain your answer.

9 If Jesus were to judge you today, would you be right with God? Explain your answer.

10 How many will eventually recognize Jesus as King and bow down? What group of people are left out of this?

11 When Jesus is described by John in Revelation, does this description comfort or trouble you? Explain your answer.

12 What description most stands out to you from these passages?

13 Do these descriptions have a basis in any other Scripture?

14 How should we think of Jesus today: the human Jesus who walked the earth or the glorified Jesus on a throne in heaven? Explain your answer.

NOTES

HOW TO USE THIS STUDY
IN A CLASSROOM

This study is designed for the individual at home, but it can also be used for classroom purposes. Most congregations that might use this book are set up on a thirteen-week class schedule, and we designed this workbook to work in that setting.

The first class, when you pass out the book, can be an open discussion on the "Pre-Study Questions." We designed these questions to help the individual (and the teacher) know where they are in their understanding of the topic. This will guide the study and hopefully create some personal goals and objectives for what will be learned in the class.

The students can then engage in the lesson throughout the week, beginning their week with the lesson overview reading, doing their daily readings and questions, and coming together with the class to do the "Deeper Thinking Questions." Hopefully, the students have been diligent in their readings and have already thought through some of these questions for class discussion.

When we wrote this series, we aimed to help students develop a daily habit of being in God's Word. As a teacher, please strongly emphasize this necessity. The student will certainly learn from this book and by opening God's Word, but the greatest thing they can learn is a personal dependency on God through His Word. The more we can do to emphasize that, the better.

We pray that your students will grow and ask deep questions about the Bible. We pray that you will grow as a teacher and help these students to feel comfortable asking hard questions. The more we can discuss the truth and turn these students to the source of truth, the better prepared they will be for a world that will want them to question the truth. Multiple studies have proven that those with a Biblical worldview and who regularly access God's Word are more productive, happier, and fulfilled than those who do not. We want what is best for these students, and we know that begins with their eyes on God's Word and on Jesus. Thank you for your role as a teacher and for providing that guidance for them.

Made in the USA
Middletown, DE
02 February 2025